Three Minutes to
Blues, Rock, and Folk Harmonica

by David Harp

I dedicate this book to my father, Fred — a New York city firefighter — and to all of his comrades, living and dead, who have sacrificed their own safety to make "The City" a safer place for the rest of us. Also to my mother, Frieda — poet, nurse, deep spirit — without whom Fred could not have done his job, nor I mine.

ISBN 0-918321-77-8

© David Harp's musical i press, 2002

Illustrated by Katherine Feldman

Recording Engineer: Gus Ziesing

Anatomical Diagrams by Don Mayne

Thanks to Lily for her Song Help

A Few Other Books by David Harp

- Blues & Rock Harmonica Made Easy • The Three Minute Meditator*
- Music Theory Made Easy • The Pocket Harmonica Songbook • Instant Flute
- Three Minutes to Blues Harmonica: The Video • Metaphysical Fitness*
- Bending the Blues • Instant Guitar • Country & Western Harmonica Made Easy
- Music Theory Made Easy for Harmonica • Instant Blues Harmonica (Vol. I & II)
- Instant Chromatic Harmonica • The Instant Harmonica Kit for Kids
- How To Whistle Like A Pro • Make Me Musical: Instant Harmonica
- The Three Minute Meditator Audiotape* • Me and My Harmonica
- How To Save Your Back, Neck, & Shoulders In Ten Minutes A Day • EarthCards
- The New Three Minute Meditator* • Instant Harmonica for Kids (Video)
- The Instant Rhythm Kit • How to Fight a Cold & Win
- Blues, Rock, and Jazz Improvising Made Easy • And more coming...

(* written with my beloved twin sister, Dr. Nina Smiley-Feldman)

List of Songs and Solos

Table of Contents

This book is divided into "tracks." Each track of the book corresponds to one track of the recording — the book is not meant to be used by itself!

(So if you don't have the recording, please go to page 93 now.)

Read This First: Listen and Learn!

This method is actually based more on learning by listening, than on learning by reading. So feel free to read only the "Boxed" sections on pages 5 and 6, then put this book aside right now and start listening to the recording. You can just come back and glance at the book when you *hear* me suggest it.

New to harmonica? Check out the "Harmonica Care" section on page 91. It'll lengthen life — of the harmonica, at least!

Track 1: Introduction

Hi! I'm David Harp. For many years, I considered myself tone-deaf — until I learned to play the harmonica, that is. Now, playing Blues*, rock, and folk "harp" has become an important and incredibly satisfying part of my daily life.

Although most of my formal training is in the field of cognitive psychology — the study of how the brain processes information — I've also taught more than half a million people to blow their blues away. By doing this over many years, through private lessons, large group workshops, books, and recordings, I've developed what I believe is the fastest and easiest harmonica method ever. And you're looking at it!

* Note: I always capitalize the word "Blues" — apologies to grammarians — to show my respect and appreciation of the original masters who gave us this musical gift.

Three Minutes to Harmonica? Skeptical?

Before I learned to play, if someone had told me that I could learn to play even a little bit of harp in just three minutes, I'd have called them a liar (unless they were lots bigger than me). In fact, it took me about thirty hours of practice to play my first feeble version of a folk song, and six months of daily playing to learn even the most elementary of Blues "riffs."

So perhaps you wonder how I can teach people to play in just a few minutes. But if you can breathe in and breathe out when you want to, and feed yourself safely with a fork, you already have most of the *physical* skills that you're going to need. And I'll provide the mental and musical ones.

How to Use This Method

Some people prefer to learn by reading, others by listening. I've got both strategies covered in this method, but you will have to do some of each!

Most of the information you need is on the recording. But certain things — like learning to hold the harmonica — are easier to learn by looking than by listening. You're welcome if you like, to read every word on every page. But for fastest results, simply listen to the recording and take a peek at this book whenever you hear me suggest it. You can always come back later and read those sections that most interest you.

> For your convenience, I'll put the most crucial written information inside a box like this, so it will stand out.
>
> To keep the material organized, both the book and the recording are divided into *"Tracks."* The written material in Track 1 of the book relates to Track 1 of the recording, and so on.

> In general: any time you want or need more details about something you've heard on the recording, turn to the same track number in this book. Need help with the Chicago Blues Breathing Pattern in Track 4 of the recording? Just turn to Track 4 of the book, and check out the notation for it!

This way, if you *don't* choose to read every word, just look at each illustration and check out the boxes. There won't be too many boxes, since almost everything that's truly important to know is already on the recording!

Extra Goodies: The "More Great Stuff" Section

I also include some interesting but not absolutely essential extra material in the book. For example, some of you might be interested in my use of harmonica to teach cognitive psychology skills to corporations, chronically-ill children, and frail elderly people, or to enhance aerobic endurance in college athletes (check out my website for info on that — www.davidharp.com). If this doesn't intrigue you, just skip it!

In the section entitled "More Great Stuff," I'll provide you with lots of extra songs in a variety of styles, all written out in my incredibly easy to use harmonica notation system, plus instructions on harmonica care, how to play with other people, and other...great stuff!

Enough Reading for Now

It's time to stop reading, turn on the recording, and go on to Track Two, my famous "Three Minute Harmonica Lesson"! It will teach you everything you need to know to begin enjoying the most entertaining, creative and satisfying hobby that I've ever encountered!

Track 2: 3 Minutes to Harmonica

In some ways, this is the most important track in the book
and recording. It contains all of the basic harmonica skills
that you'll need to get started. I'll keep it short and simple.
As always, listen to the recording, and just look at the
pictures and the boxed sections in the book.

Take a Good Look

> Note: Some people wash their
> harp before they play (page 91).

Your harmonica should have ten holes, with a number from
one to ten above each hole, and a little letter "C" on it. (This
means you have a harmonica in "the key of C" — page 88.) If
yours doesn't look *more or less* like this, please go to page 92 now.

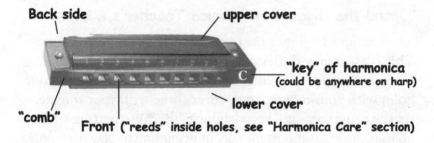

Back side

upper cover

"key" of harmonica
(could be anywhere on harp)

lower cover

"comb"

Front ("reeds" inside holes, see "Harmonica Care" section)

How to Hold Your Harmonica: The "Fork Hold"

You've been practicing this
for years, every time you eat
or write! Just make sure
that the holes are facing your
mouth (duh!) and that the little
numbers are on top.

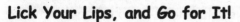

Lick Your Lips, and Go for It!

Breathe in and out through your harmonica.
Lick your lips (to reduce friction) and slide around. Play the
low number holes and the high ones, like I do on the recording.

The Biggest Beginner's Mistake...

...is not having the harmonica deep enough inside your mouth! Don't be afraid to eat the "tin sandwich" — cover at least three holes at a time. That's a normal and comfortable mouth open position, just like when we are talking.

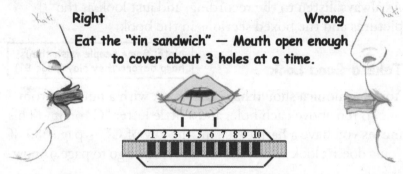

Right

Wrong

Eat the "tin sandwich" — Mouth open enough to cover about 3 holes at a time.

...And the Biggest Harmonica Teacher's Mistake

...is making a beginner try to play one single hole at a time. This is especially difficult to do using the old-fashioned German "tongue blocking" method, in which you cover four holes with your mouth, then cover three with your tongue. As the gangsters say, "Fagedaboutit!" Because getting single holes is the least important part of beginning to play harmonica.

Notes and Chords

A note is a single musical sound. Each of the ten little holes on your harmonica will produce **one note on the in breath, and another note on the out breath.** *"Chords"* are two or more notes that are "in harmony" — that is, they sound good when played together.

In fact, our instrument is called the harmonica ("harmony-ca") because the notes are always in harmony — no matter how many we play at one time. Even if you cover five or six holes with your mouth and breathe, you'll get a great sounding chord. But don't put the whole thing inside your mouth. I did that once to demonstrate a ten hole chord, and it got stuck — embarrassing!

Ready! Aim! Play!

Now you're ready to play along with my verbal instructions. I'll tell you which holes to aim your mouth at, when to breathe in, and when to breathe out. It's as simple as that!

Just aim your slightly opened mouth at the hole numbers that I describe. Don't worry too much about which holes you are covering — the timing of the in and out breaths are the most important thing!

Don't worry at all about playing one hole at a time — we'll mostly be playing *"chords"* (three holes at a time). So if I name three holes (like 4, 5, and 6), just aim your mouth at the middle one of the three numbers (the 5 hole). If your mouth is slightly open, the 4 hole and the 6 hole will be covered, too. For example, try playing these chords right now:

in chord on **456**   **out** chord on **456**
(Inhale)   **(Exhale)**

If you like, spend a few seconds using the tip of your tongue to explore the size of the holes of the harmonica and the dividers between them. Using your tongue will help you control how many holes you cover, and help you center your mouth on the hole you want.

The Beauty of Breathing Patterns

They're easy, and they work. I believe that my Breathing Pattern method of teaching is the fastest way to get a total beginner to play Blues and rock music on the harmonica.

Why do they work so well? Because these Breathing Patterns approximate the notes of the *"Blues Scale,"* upon which most Blues and rock music is based. But don't worry about that for now — it's advanced stuff!

Steady Beat and the "Count of Four"

This is easier to hear than to read about. The "Count" helps you be ready to start playing at exactly the right time. In this case, we'll use a "Count of Four." This means that you'll start playing when you would expect me to say the word "five." Some styles of music use a count of three, or five, as you'll see.

Your First Breathing Pattern: "In—Out—In—Silence"

Try to tap your foot as you play — it'll help you to maintain a steady beat even when not playing (like during the "silent" beat).

in   **out**   **in**   (silent beat)

in   **out**   **in**   (silent beat)

Keep your harmonica *way* in between your lips when playing.

Don't let air escape through nose when playing.

Don't worry about getting single holes, just aim your lips at the numbers I ask you to play.

Make sure you understand Breathing Patterns, or go back and practice them more.

Track 3: Blues, Rock, or Folk?

If you can play the In-Out-In-Silence Breathing Pattern from Track Two, you're ready for anything! (If you can't, go back to Track Two and practice breathing with me for a few minutes, or up to Track Seven for some extra help.)

Like Blues music? Go straight to Track Four for a simple but satisfying Chicago-Style Blues *"Riff"* — based on a Breathing Pattern, of course.

> What's a riff? Just a short combination of notes or chords that we like, and memorize. Then we can use it again and again. Most of the riffs that I'll teach you are based on my Breathing Patterns.

Prefer rock and roll? Go to Track Five, and learn a "Boogie Woogie," the foundation upon which thousands of rock songs are based.

Or go to Track Six, for your first folk song. This will eventually lead you to play many different musical styles: Celtic music, Gypsy music (or more correctly and politely, *Rom* music), Sea Chanteys, and even Classical music (much of which is actually based on older folk tunes).

But first, two hints:

> This method is organized so that you can learn only the styles of music that you like best. But: learning Blues and rock music will teach you breath control that will help you to play better folk music. And learning folk music will teach you note control that will help you to play better Blues and rock...

> You don't *need* to learn my harmonica notation system now, even though it will only take a minute to do so. Later on, when working with more advanced songs and riffs, it's likely to come in handy...

The Easiest Notation System

Yes, you can learn a song or riff just by listening to it. But being able to see what it looks like written down can be a big help, especially for those who are visual learners.

Fortunately, I won't make you learn the musical language known as "standard notation" — that complicated-looking written music composed of lots of little lines full of funny-shaped notes and strange words.

Instead, my notation system is so simple that you've just about learned it already, simply by playing along with my vocal instructions on the recording in Track Two. Here it is.

Which Hole Numbers to Cover?

I'll write down the hole numbers that I want you to cover with your mouth. If I write down the numbers four, five, and six — you put your mouth over those holes (not exactly rocket science, is it?). A line under the numbers reminds you to play them all at the same time, as a chord.

The <u>456</u> Chord

I write <u>456</u>, your mouth covers these holes!

4 5 6

Breathe In or Breathe Out?

If I want you to breathe out, I'll write the numbers in outlined type. If I want you to breathe in, I'll write the numbers in **filled in** type. So...

345 means breathe out on holes 3, 4, and 5.

123 means breathe in on holes 1, 2, and 3.

How Long to Play it For?

I'll show you how long to hold each beat for, just as I did in Track Two when I taught you your first breathing pattern. But instead of using little foot cartoons, I'll use dots, to keep it simple. Each dot represents one beat.

Putting It Together...

Here's the In-Out-In-Silence Breathing Pattern on the holes four, five, and six from Track Two, in my notation.

•
456 • •
456 456 (silent beat)

Numbers tell you which holes to cover with your mouth.

A line under two or more numbers reminds you to play them all at the same time (as a chord).

Each dot • represents one beat.

outlined means breathe *out*.

filled in means breathe *in*.

If you can read the In-Out-In-Silence Breathing Pattern just above, you've got it!

Track 4: The Chicago Blues Breathing Pattern

As I introduce this track you'll hear my guitarist and me in the background, playing a style of music called the *"Twelve Bar Blues."* He provides the structure based on a specific series of guitar chords played with a Blues rhythm. Doing this is often called *"playing a chord structure,"* or *"playing a chord progression."* And I add a harmonica solo, consisting of six versions of what I call the Chicago Breathing Pattern riff — you'll learn this yourself, in a moment.

> The *Twelve Bar Blues* is the most popular general type of blues, and is often used in rock and jazz and pop music, too.

So it's worth listening to this intro a few times, just to get the feel of it. If you're interested in music theory, or plan to play with other musicians, read the above paragraph and check out page 90 for info on the chords of the Twelve Bar Blues.

The Chicago Blues Breathing Pattern

I've developed a Breathing Pattern that works beautifully with many styles of music, although I originally began using it to teach my students to play simple harp riffs in the style of Chicago blues musicians. I'll write it out for you: first as the general Breathing Pattern (just ins and outs), then as you'd play it on the holes four, five, and six. Make the breathing changes from in to out to in crisp, almost percussive!

• • •   •   •   • • •
innnn **out** **in**   **(three silent beats)**

• • •   • • •   • • •   • • •
456 **456** **456**   **Each riff is 8 beats — count the dots!**

Your First Chicago Blues Verse

Practice playing this eight beat riff a few times. Then play it six times along with my Blues background music, to form one *"verse"* of a Blues! It's not a terribly exciting verse — a bit repetitive, perhaps — but with a good Blues band and a big amplifier, it wouldn't sound half bad!

This verse is 48 beats long (8 beats times 6 riffs), which makes it a Twelve Bar Blues Verse, since Blues musicians often refer to four beats of music as *"one bar."*

Movin' It Around!

What's the best thing about my Breathing Pattern method? Once you learn the pattern, you can use it anywhere!

Demonstrate this for yourself by playing the Chicago Breathing Pattern on the holes 5, 6, and 7. Then on holes 6, 7, and 8. Then (although a bit shrill for most tastes), on holes 8, 9, and 10. You now know four different Chicago Blues Riffs!

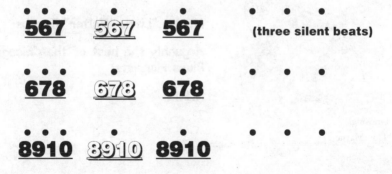

In the second verse, you won't just repeat the same riff six times. Instead, you'll form a more varied twelve bar solo by putting together three different riffs. As with the first verse, you'll play a two bar (eight beat) riff six times to form this second twelve bar (48 beat) blues verse.

Your Second Chicago Blues Verse

You'll use the Chicago Breathing Pattern on holes 4, 5, and 6, on holes 6, 7, and 8, and on holes 8, 9, and 10.

I'll talk you right through this verse using the words:

"Play it in the middle!" for the 456 riff...

"A couple holes higher!" for the 678 riff, and the words

"Way up high!" for the 8910 riff.

Don't worry about exactly which holes you're on — just feel the beat and give it a try. I'm very forgiving, and so is the harmonica! Pull out your harmonica and play this solo along with your neighbor's garage band, and your friends who never heard you play before will be very impressed indeed!

Marion "Little Walter" Jacobs

Arguably the best of the Chicago Blues Harpists.

R.I.P.

Drawing:
Don Mayne

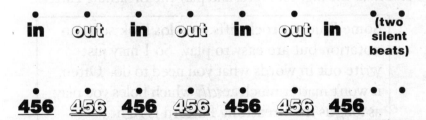

Track 5: The Boogie Woogie Breathing Pattern

"Boogie Woogie" or "Barrelhouse Blues" music was born perhaps a century ago, where the Mississippi River runs into the Gulf of Mexico. These often lively and upbeat "Delta Blues" styles came up the river before the Second World War, and developed into the usually slower and sadder Chicago Blues styles (which you've already begun to learn).

A great deal of classic and modern rock music uses the Boogie Woogie as a foundation. And as you probably know, most modern American music — rock, jazz, soul, punk, and rap — owes a tremendous debt to those early African-American originators of the Blues. Anyone who loves music must pay homage to these original masters, who gave the world many of its greatest forms of artistic self-expression, with so little recognition or reward!

The Boogie Woogie Breathing Pattern

Listen a few times before trying it on the 4, 5, and 6 hole, then make the changes fast and crisp. Repeat this two bar (eight beat) Breathing Pattern until it feels familiar!

in	out	in	out	in	out	in	(two silent beats)

456	456	456	456	456	456	456	

The last "out-in" part is tricky for some, so I'll describe it in more detail on the next page.

The Boogie Woogie Beat

Notice that the last *"out-in"* is squashed into a single beat.

in　out　in　out　in　out　in　(two silent beats)

If this confuses you, listen to my foot taps. The last out breath happens just as my foot hits the floor. The last in breath happens as my foot comes back up, but ends just before my foot taps again to represent the first of the two silent beats. I show this visually by having a dot over the out breath, and no dot over the in.

Movin' It Around

Just like we did with the Chicago Breathing Pattern, we'll practice using the Boogie Woogie Breathing Pattern on holes 6, 7, and 8, and then on holes 8, 9, and 10.

678　678　678　678　678　678　678

I won't write the 8, 9, and 10 hole version out in notation — it looks harder than it is (too many numbers). Just aim your mouth at the highest holes, and play the Breathing Pattern.

> Some Blues or rock riffs or solos look scary in notation but are easy to play. So I may just write out in words what you need to do. Often, it won't matter much *exactly* which holes you play, as long as the Breathing Pattern is right...

Two Boogie Woogie Blues Verses

Now you're ready to play along with my blues band — bass, drums, and rhythm guitar. Aim your mouth at holes 4, 5, and 6, and get ready for the first in breath at the count of four!

Your First Boogie Woogie Verse

In the first verse, just repeat the Boogie Woogie Breathing Pattern six times on the 4, 5, and 6 holes.

Just repeat the following line six times (6 two bar riffs = 12 Bars)

456 4̶5̶6̶ **456** 4̶5̶6̶ **456** 4̶5̶6̶ **456** (two silent beats)

Remember to stay empty enough during the two beats of silence so that you can start the next riff on an in breath.

Your Second Boogie Woogie Verse

I'll talk you through it, using the Boogie Woogie Breathing Pattern to play riffs on the 4, 5, and 6 holes, the 6, 7, and 8 holes, and the 8, 9, and 10 holes. You'll combine these three riffs to play a more exciting Boogie Woogie Twelve Bar Blues Verse!

Important: This *looks* way harder than it is to *play!*

456 4̶5̶6̶ **456** 4̶5̶6̶ **456** 4̶5̶6̶ **456**

456 4̶5̶6̶ **456** 4̶5̶6̶ **456** 4̶5̶6̶ **456**

678 6̶7̶8̶ **678** 6̶7̶8̶ **678** 6̶7̶8̶ **678**

456 4̶5̶6̶ **456** 4̶5̶6̶ **456** 4̶5̶6̶ **456**

8910 8̶9̶1̶0̶ **8910** 8̶9̶1̶0̶ **8910** 8̶9̶1̶0̶ **8910**

456 4̶5̶6̶ **456** 4̶5̶6̶ **456** 4̶5̶6̶ **456**

Great Playalong Hint: Does your sound system have a stereo balance control? In many of the recorded exercises that have background music, you can get rid of either my voice (usually on the right), my harmonica (usually on the left), or sometimes both, by using the left/right balance control.

Track 6: Your First Folk Song

In this track you won't just learn how to play your first folk song. You'll also find that you don't have to be a highly experienced harmonica player to express emotion through your instrument. In addition, you'll begin to learn to navigate your way around the harmonica, hole by hole. This will help you to play more interesting folk, Blues, and rock songs.

Navigation: The Hole Thing

Follow the instructions on the recording, and practice locating the holes 3, 4, 5, and 6. This does not — repeat not — mean that I want you to play them as single notes. It merely means that I want you to be able to *aim* your lips at the center of each hole (while covering the holes on either side) with some degree of confidence.

Aim, don't obsess!
Start empty —   **3   4   5   6**
all OUT notes!

Practice, take your time, and don't be self-critical. As I said, the same hand/mouth coordination that allows you to safely feed yourself with a pointy fork will help you to do this, with just a bit of work.

Taps: Lots of Emotion, Not Much Technique

This lovely campfire song is traditionally used to express a range of wistful or sad emotion, from noting the end of a great day outdoors as you sit around the embers of the campfire, to mourning a fallen comrade. It's easy to play, using just four notes, all on the out breath — but play it with feeling. It's never too soon to start expressing your feelings through the harmonica. Simple as it is, it's one of my favorite, and most often requested, songs...

From now on, I'll usually write out a song using single notes instead of chords — mainly to save space, and because it looks less cluttered.

You'll still use the *"aim technique."* Just aim your mouth at the single hole I write down, but keep it slightly open, to include the holes on each side. This'll give you the right chords to play the song.

Songs often sound better when played with chords, or a combination of single holes and chords, than if played with single holes only.

Taps

Taps starts at the count of three, not four, so listen to me play it, then join me. Start with your lungs fairly full, and catch a quick breath whenever you need to (the silent beats provide you with lots of time to do this). Notice that many of the notes occur *in between* the beats — while your foot is up in the air. These are the notes that do not have a dot over them.

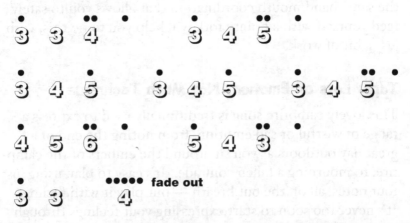

Catch a quick breath whenever you
need to — they're all OUT notes!

Catching Your Breath, and Wooziness

You'll often need to catch a quick in or out breath when playing. Obviously, if your lungs are getting too full, you'll have to let some air out. And if you're getting too empty, you'll have to get some air in. Most songs or riffs have silent beats that you can catch a breath during. Sometimes you'll even have to catch a quick one between notes.

> The easiest way to catch a quick breath is to drop your lower lip about 1/4 inch, and grab the breath from *under* the harmonica! This won't make an unwanted sound, and it won't take your mouth away from the hole that you're on! And if you ever feel woozy while playing, read on.

No matter what shape you are in, playing harmonica is likely to make you use more air than you're used to. This can produce a little bit of wooziness. If it does, just take a break for a minute. After a week or so, you'll have to play really hard to get woozy. I like to play as I run (and have a whole program on "Harmonica-robic™" conditioning). Sometimes I even get a bit spacey, especially if I'm going fast on an uphill!

Improv Versus Note-for-Note

In Blues and rock, there's room to be creative with the notes you use — that's just improvisation, or making up your own riffs as you play! But when playing folk or classical songs (especially songs that listeners may know), it's important to aim in the right vicinity, and to keep track of the ins and outs.

> Some people like to look at the notation while listening to me play the song. Others learn a song best from hearing it, without notation. Some would rather play from the notation than from my verbal instructions. Suit yourself!

Track 7: More on Beat and Breathing Patterns

I would like to mention that a good sense of rhythm is not something that most of us are born with. Rather, it can be learned by tapping and even counting beats along with music as you listen, or by paying attention to the rhythm of your feet as you walk. Don't be embarrassed to do these things — I do both on a daily basis to keep my sense of timing in shape.

Obviously, developing a good sense of rhythm is one of those things that's better learned by listening and doing than by reading about. So if you have trouble tapping your foot in time with me, or if you can't seem to maintain the Breathing Patterns, this track (of the recording) will help more than anything I write here.

If you've had trouble with the Breathing Patterns in Track 2, it will be worth your while to read all of this track. Otherwise, just skim it.

Bars and Measures

Blues, rock, and other types of musicians often break a rhythm pattern into chunks of four beats each, called *"bars"* or *"measures."* Count some along with me, and count some while walking, too.

Breathing Pattern Review

Have you had problems with the Breathing Patterns? If you have, I've provided extra help in the recording for this track. The following written hints and details may also help.

**Remember: 1) Outlined Means Breathe OUT!
2) When in doubt, listen to the recording!**

The Ins and Outs of Breathing

Since we're used to talking on the out breath only, we're very used to paying attention to the use of the out breath. We just grab a quick inhale as needed, so that we can talk some more.

Also, since we always talk on the out breath, we usually start a sentence by taking an in breath beforehand. But many of the Breathing Patterns start on an in breath, so we need to be at least somewhat (or sometimes very) empty as we begin.

For these reasons, we harp players must develop more control of our in breaths as well. In fact, we have to control both the inhale and exhales — we can't just breathe in or out as we please anymore!

Practice some "in - out - in" breaths without the harmonica. Pay close attention to how it feels, in your lungs, your mouth, your stomach muscles. As I said on the recording, focus on the breath is a mainstay of many of the world's contemplative traditions — so it's a very relaxing, even spiritual, thing to do!

Close the Nose, Open the Mind

Try not to lose air through your nose as you play — that's as big a waste as self-critical thoughts when you hit a sour note during a song! I'll give you more instruction on nose closing in the next track.

Now, if you need Breathing Pattern practice, work along with my detailed instructions for this "in-out-in-beat" Breathing Pattern on the recording.

456   456   456 (silent beat)

Now go back to Track Three if you came here from Track Two to get extra help, or go on to Track Eight.

Track 8: Harmonica Tone and Special Effects

As I wrote at the beginning of Track Seven, some things are better heard than read. Harmonica tone effects are among them. But that doesn't mean that harmonica tone is not important, and there are years of work in this track — I still work on my tone and special effects every day! By the way: the music you hear as I introduce this track is based on the "Dirty Dirty Dog" pattern described later on in this track, combined with some more advanced "bending" techniques (also described later).

Wide Open Spaces

The more open space there is in your mouth and throat, the better tone you'll have. Keeping open space in the mouth is simply a matter of keeping your tongue relaxed and low in the mouth as you play, and your teeth at least slightly apart. See page 54 for more on this...

Keeping open space in your throat, which I define as going down as far as the stomach, is harder, but can offer great benefits.

Deeper Breathing

Try to breathe from your stomach. What does that mean? Well, many of us tend to breathe shallowly, using mostly the muscles of our chest rather than the dinner-plate shaped diaphragm muscle that separates our lungs from our other internal organs. When we breathe in, the diaphragm flexes downward, pulling air down into our lungs. When we breathe out, it flexes upwards, pushing the air up and out.

Stomach Breathing Exercise

Here's an exercise that will help you to focus your attention on breathing from the stomach. Stand in a relaxed position, both hands on your stomach. As you breathe in, gently expand your belly — you'll be able to feel it bulging out with your hands. As you breathe out, contract your stomach muscles, so that your stomach becomes flatter. (I don't say flat because mine never is, anymore!) If this feels un-natural — the opposite of how you usually breathe — you're probably a "chest-breather."

By gently practicing this exercise, you'll improve both your breathing and your tone! Harmonica playing can really help your respiration — if this interests you, see the "Where To Go from Here" section on my book *Better Breathing Through Harmonica,* used by rehab facilities in various parts of the nation!

Close the Nose!

Most of us never consciously use the muscles of our soft palate (at the back of the throat) to close the nasal passage and separate our nose from our mouth.

So just think of blowing out birthday candles to keep your nose shut on the out breaths. Think of drinking a thickshake through a straw to keep your nose shut while inhaling. Feel those throat muscles tighten!

Attack that Harp!

Soft and hard, flowing and sharp, sliding gently from place to place or starting each sound with an aggressive puff of air — there are many different ways to play even a single chord.

> This is all on the recording, so listen and you'll begin to develop your own style of "harp attack."

Articulation

Articulation is nothing more than a fancy name for *whispering* words like "duh" or "tuh" through the harmonica. Whispering (not *saying*) multiple "duh duh duh duh" sequences is an easy way to break a note or chord into lots of short, sharp, pieces.

It's much easier to do all of these articulations on the out breaths. But if you start empty and simply make your tongue and lips go through the same whispering motions, you'll get the in-articulations. Took me years of practice, to do it really well.

The Dirty Dirty Dogs: Classical Versus Swing!

The four beat "Dirty Dirty Dog" is one of my very favorite articulations, as described in detail on the recording. Here are the "Non-Swinging" Dirty Dogs (as a classical musician would say them, if classical musicians did, which they don't).

Non-Swinging: European Musical Tradition
(Each divided beat broken into two equal parts)

Dir   tee   Dir   tee   Dog   (silent)

It's much more fun if you "swing" the Dirty Dog rhythm. The bold syllables are emphasized, as you'll hear on the recording.

Swinging: African-American Musical Tradition
(The "downbeat" part of a divided beat held longer than the "upbeat")

Dirrr   d'   Dirrr   d'   Dog   (silent)

Whisper it in the middle of the harmonica. If I want you to use a specific articulation, I'll write it above the notes. In swing beats, I'll make the upbeats (shorter parts) smaller.

dirrr   d'   dirrr   d'   dog
456   456   456   456   456   (silent)

Puttin' Out the Dogs

Start on the out breath, and whisper some Dirty Dirty Dogs forcefully in different places on the harp: low, middle, high.

Then lick your lips and move or slide the harmonica during a Dirty Dirty Dog. Start low and end high, or start high and end low, or move around during this articulation in any way you can think of.

Don't worry about reproducing this exact riff — just start in the middle, and head up towards the high holes. Then work your way back down.

dirrr	d'	dirrr	d'	dog	•
456	456	**567**	567	**678**	(silent)

dirrr	d'	dirrr	d'	dog	•
789	789	**567**	567	**456**	(silent)

Doggin' It In

Unfortunately, you also need to do the Dirty Dogs on the in breaths. Start empty, keep your nose shut, and just start doing it, odd as it may feel. Once you can do an in Dirty Dirty Dog in one place, lick your lips and move it around!

dirrr	d'	dirrr	d'	dog	•
456	456	**567**	567	**678**	(silent)

dirrr	d'	dirrr	d'	dog	•
789	789	**567**	567	**456**	(silent)

But don't get hung up here — spend a minute on the in Dogs, then come back to them later (for the next few weeks). In the meantime, go on to Track 9, in both book and recording.

Track 9: Slidin', Shakin', Doggin', and some Crucial Advice

As I say in the intro to this track, *perfecting* the material in Technique Tracks Seven, Eight, and Nine could easily take years of work. The music behind my voice consists mostly of alternating in and out Dirty Dogs, with slides and shakes added, and ending (did you recognize it?) with a Chicago riff.

Sliding and Shaking

There's not much to say in writing about the slide effect, except: keep your lips wet! However, this picture of the hand movement for the shake effect — back and forth sideways about 1/4 of an inch, moving from the wrist, not the elbow — may be useful.

The shake will feel awkward at first, but it gets easier as the neurons of your brain memorize the hand movement. Soon it'll be as easy as brushing your teeth! Apply the shake to the Chicago and Boogie Woogie Breathing Patterns, as in my recorded examples, to create some great riffs!

• • •   •   •   • • •

456   **456**   **456**   **(three silent beats)**
wwwwwwwwwwwwwwww

• • • • • • •   • •

456 **456** **456** **456** **456** **456** **456**
wwwwwwwwwwwwwwwwwwwwwwwwwwwwwwwwwwwwwwwwwww

I put a wavy line under chords that I want you to shake on.

When you can add a "bending" effect to a shake — as I do while talking about "...a good shake takes a long time to develop" — you'll be playing pro-level harp (at least for a riff or two)!

Dirty Dog Effects

Now it's time to combine some of the special effects with the Dirty Dirty Dog articulation. Practice shaking some dogs, alternating a bar of in Dirty Dogs with a bar of out Dirty Dogs, as in my recorded example using only the middle holes.

Try playing the Dirty Dirty in the middle, and the Dog a hole or two higher, or a hole or two lower. Here's the example I used for this, with a shake on the second and third beat of the in part:

Dirr	d'	Dirr	d'	Dog	
•		•		•	•
345	**345**	**345**	**345**	**456**	

wwwwwwwwwwwwwwwwwww   **In Dogs!**

Dirr	d'	Dirr	d'	Dog	
•		•		•	•
345	**345**	**345**	**345**	**234**	

Out Dogs!

Movin' the Dirty Dog Riffs

You can move during your entire Dirty Dirty Dog too, as I do in my example, going up on the ins, then back down on the outs. Don't try to play just what I do — instead, make up any variation you like on this!

Dirr	d'	Dirr	d'	Dog	
•		•		•	•
345	**345**	**456**	**456**	**789**	

In Dogs!

Dirr	d'	Dirr	d'	Dog	
•		•		•	•
567	**567**	**345**	**345**	**234**	

Out Dogs!

Slidin' the Dirty Dog Riffs — Mine and Yours

Slide those Dogs, too! My sliding example consists of two bars, first in, then out. For the in bar, I slide from low to high for each Dirr, and back down for each d', ending with a low to high in slide for the Dog.

For the out bar, I slide low to high for the first Dirr, then do the d' up high, another Dirr d' in the middle, and the dog down low. Once again, these are suggestions to help you create your own riffs. I won't write them down, as I *don't* want you to dutifully memorize and repeat them (unless you want to).

The Dirty Dog Rock

After you've done your Dog work, apply what you've learned by playing them along with a popular style of classic rock and roll, which I call *"Two Bar Two Chord Rock."* Some of my favorite rock musicians, from Donovan to J. Geils, use this particular chord structure or chord progression.

In this style of music the guitar and bass player alternate two chords, for one bar each, so the pattern repeats itself every two bars. One chord (the "G chord") fits in very well with the *inhaled* Dirty Dogs. The other chord ("C7 chord") fits in with the *exhaled* Dirty Dogs.

There are many other riffs that can be played along with this type of rock music (and I'll throw a few "non-Dog" riffs in at the end). But for now stick with the Dirty Dogs, alternating one bar of in Dogs with one bar of out Dogs. However, I mostly want you to learn the Dogs as a rhythm exercise — we'll use the Dog rhythm in a more interesting way in Track 20.

If you like this style of music, come back to it and play along. Remember: if you have a stereo system with a left/right control, you can lose my voice and harmonica. Oh — and the verbal advice I offer towards the end of this track is, in my humble opinion, the most important part of this method...

Track 10: Rockin' The Blues

In the intro to this track, I demonstrate two things. First, while the band plays a Twelve Bar Boogie Woogie Blues in the background, I alternate Boogie Woogie Breathing Patterns with Chicago Breathing Patterns — and it sounds great, simple though my riffs are. Second, as we just did with the Dirty Dirty Dogs, I move around *during* my Boogie Woogie and Chicago Breathing Patterns.

Shakin' and Movin' the Boogie Woogie

You have already, I hope, practiced using your shake *during* a Boogie Woogie Breathing Pattern. Now it's time to add some movement, too. So lick your lips and move while you play this great Breathing Pattern, which I'll write down right here for your convenience.

in out in out in out in (silent beats)

Try playing along with my example, more or less: Start one in the middle, and end up at the high end. Then start the next one at the high end, and finish it off in the middle. I won't write these out — I'd rather that you create your own variations.

Improvise! Create Your Own Riffs!

Once you learn to move around during a Breathing Pattern, you are improvising — creating your own music as you play! No longer are you playing riffs of mine. Instead, you're coming up with riffs of your own, since only you can choose where and how and when to move. Although I love to play riffs composed by the master players, and love to play songs of all types, there is no more creative and free way of making music than improvisation! Enjoy!

The Two Hole Chord

Now might be a good time to start playing some chords with just two holes. To do this, you'll have to aim your mouth a bit differently. Use your tongue to identify the divider between holes 4 and 5. Then aim your mouth at that divider, while puckering your lips out just a little. This will make the opening of your mouth a slightly smaller, so if you aim at the 4/5 divider, you'll cover just the 4 and the 5 holes.

Once you get the hang of it, play some two hole Boogie Woogie Breathing Pattern riffs. A two hole shake is more dramatic and crisper than a three hole shake. Start by aiming at the divider between holes 4 and 5, and try to shake only far enough to center on 4, then on 5, as your hand moves.

A Heavy Rock Boogie

Now it's time for a duet. Alternate some Boogie Woogie Breathing Patterns with me — I'll play one, then you! We'll use a simple but dramatic *"Boogie"* for background music (not to be confused with a Boogie Woogie).

A Boogie Woogie is a specific type of Twelve Bar Blues chord structure or chord progression (as described on pages 14 and 90). A Boogie is a blues/rock style that doesn't "progress" from chord to chord (so it's not a chord progression) but just stays in the same chord, with a heavy, almost menacing rhythm. Bands like Canned Heat, Z.Z. Top, and the great, late, blues rocker John Lee Hooker often play in this style.

My verbal instructions will help you, if you need it. If you like, try to play what I do. Or try to play something similar — perhaps with the same effects, but a different movement of the harmonica. Or just get ideas from listening to my riffs, and improvise — see what comes out!

If you like this Boogie style, you've got a treat coming in Track 20. Use your stereo control to lose my voice or harp.

Track 11: Movin' to Chicago

We did it with the Dirty Dogs. We did it with the Boogie
Woogie. Now it's time to start moving *during* the Chicago
Breathing Pattern. My favorite way to do this is to move only
once, just before the last in breath.

The Main Chicago Riff

Here's a great sounding example, used so often that I call it
the "Main" Chicago riff (my name for it, not everyone's). I
usually shake it during the long in breath, but you could shake
the entire riff, as well.

456   4̶5̶6̶   **345**   **(three silent beats)**
wwwwww

Of course, you can start this riff anywhere you like (as you
remember — that's the beauty of Breathing Patterns). Try
aiming at the 6 hole, to start it. Throw in a shake, for fun.

567   5̶6̶7̶   **456**
wwwwww

The Chicago Turnaround

A *"turnaround"* is a musical announcement that one blues
verse is ending, and another about to begin. One easy and
commonly used turnaround involves nothing more complex
than an inhaled slide downward, ending on the 1 in note.

234   2̶3̶4̶   slide **1**
wwwwww

If I want you to slide between two notes, I'll write "slide"
(tricky, eh?). If the word "slide" is outlined, you breathe out
during the slide. If "slide" is filled in, breathe in during it. We
mostly use in slides, often coming — fast — after an out chord.

An Easy Single Note: the 1 In

It's relatively easy to get a single note
on the lowest hole. All you have to
do is angle the harmonica so
that the high end is away
from your face. This pushes
the low end of the harmonica
deep into your mouth —
don't be afraid to let the low end corner go right in!

A Dynamite 16 Beat Breathing Pattern

Combining the two bar Boogie Woogie Breathing Pattern
with the two bar Chicago Breathing Pattern provides us with
a great four bar Breathing Pattern that can be used to improvise along with many types of music, from Blues to rock to
Gypsy or *Rom* style.

in **out** **in** **out** **in** **out** **in**

innnnn **out** **in** (three silent beats)

On the recording, I'll help you, breath by breath, to play this
four bar Breathing Pattern along with my band's Twelve Bar
Blues verse. You'll create a solo similar to the one I played in
the intro to Track Ten.

Listen to my examples a few times before you try it, so that
you'll be prepared for the ways in which I ask you to move
the Breathing Patterns around. You'll use your new Chicago
Turnaround, from the previous page, to end the solo.

A Boogie Woogie Chicago Blues Verse

As always, the notation may look harder than the actual playing. So if you're a "listen learner," forget this page! But either way, try to use two note chords, if you can.

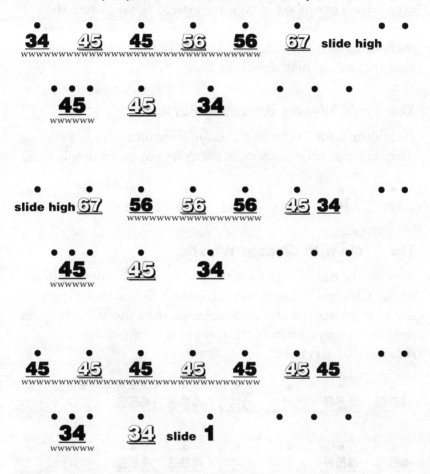

It Works Great Anywhere!

Also, at the end of this track, I'll give you a short example to demonstrate how well this four bar Breathing Pattern fits into the Rock Boogie from Track Ten, so feel free to go to the Rock Boogie Playalong Track 22 or the Boogie Woogie Playalong Track 21, and have some fun right now!

Track 12: The Rockin' Blues Train

Sometimes you just don't feel like bringing your own rock band along with you on the camping trip. Perhaps you don't even have a boombox in your backpack. That's when the train comes in handy! It's easy to play, and it sounds great without any other background music but the steady beat of your feet as you hike down the trail.

The Train Wheels Breathing Pattern

Here's the basic "Wheels" Breathing Pattern. Try it a few times without your harmonica, then play yourself a simple train.

•   •   •   •   •   •   •   •

in   in   out   out   in   in   out   out

The Train with Chicago Whistle

Play two of the Wheel Patterns on the middle holes. Then add a "Chicago Whistle" on the same holes, without losing the beat. After the three silent beats, start the Wheels again, fade the volume down as the train gets further away, and that's all there is to it!

•   •   •   •   •   •   •   •

456 456 456 456 456 456 456 456

•   •   •   •   •   •   •   •

456 456 456 456 456 456 456 456

•••   •   •   •••

456 456 456
wwwwwwwwwwwww

•   •   •   •   •   •   •   •

456 456 456 456 456 456 456 456

The Low Down Train, and the Terrible Twos!

Sad but true — the train sounds better if you play the Wheel Pattern using the low notes of the harmonica. What's the problem with that? Well, the low end of the "C" harmonica is notorious for playing hard to get, quite literally!

"My Harmonica is Broken"

I wish I had a nickel for every student in my harmonica workshops who has come up and said, "My harmonica is broken!" In about 99.5% of the cases, the problem lies in the relationship between the student's mouth and the 1, 2, and 3 in chord.

There's no way around it: the number two hole in of the "C" harmonica is hard to play. That's just the way it is, on every "C" harp made. So if the harmonica isn't far enough into your mouth — you're *sure* to get a "choked" or "funky" sound on the 1, 2, and 3 hole in chord.

Here's my test: if you can't keep the harmonica in your mouth with "no hands," it's probably not far enough in to get a good low in chord. And no, you don't have to *play* with no hands — it's just to see if your harmonica is "deep enough."

Sweet and Low: Good Tone on the Low In Chord

The recorded exercise will help you on the 1, 2, and 3 in chord. With harmonica deep in mouth and mouth as relaxed and open as possible, start on the 1, 2, and 3 out chord, then change ever so slowly and gently to the in chord. If you absolutely can't get a good tone on it, you can keep your nose open, just this once. Keep your tongue relaxed, and a "soft attack" (no articulation, low volume) — you'll get a good tone. Then you can play the out-in chords faster and more aggressively — *without* choking...

A Train to Be Proud Of

Once you've practiced getting good low end tone, and can play a low Wheels Pattern without funky tone — play a low end train with the Main Chicago Riff Whistle. It's a real crowd pleaser, especially when kids are in the crowd! Here's my recorded example, before I began talking about the troubles with 2 in...

‧123 **‧123** **‧123** **‧123** **‧123** **‧123** **‧123** **‧123**

‧123 **‧123** **‧123** **‧123** **‧123** **‧123** **‧123** **‧123**

‧‧‧45 **‧45** **34**   **‧‧‧**
wwwwwwwwwwwwww

"Chukka" That Train!

Adding a "chukka chukka" articulation on the two out breaths of the Wheels Pattern makes your train sound, well, trainier. Just whisper one chukka through each of those two out breaths "in-in-chukka-chukka." Some people find it easier to do at first *without* the harmonica — although you may want to practice *that* in private!

            chukka   chukka   chukka   chukka

‧123 **‧123** **123** **123** **‧123** **‧123** **‧123** **‧123**

            chukka   chukka   chukka   chukka

‧123 **‧123** **123** **123** **‧123** **‧123** **‧123** **‧123**

Throw in Some Train Whistles

You've already used the Chicago riff with your train. Now add a Boogie Woogie Breathing Pattern, or even a four bar Boogie Woogie plus Chicago Breathing pattern.

Just come back to the basic Wheel Pattern every so often, and you'll have an exciting balance between wild soloing and a solid rhythm section — all provided by you!

A Train Wheel Hint

When playing the train, as any good engineer would, keep a close eye on the fuel (your breath). If you start feeling too empty, either soften your out breaths or strengthen your ins. Too full? Do the reverse — softer ins, or harder outs. After some practice, you won't even have to think about it.

A Whistle Hint: Silences are Golden

Use the beats of silence at the end of the Chicago and Boogie Woogie Breathing Patterns to catch your breath if need be, and find your way back to the low in chord that begins the next Wheel Pattern. Don't forget them, and lose your rhythm!

A Train in the Brain

Once you feel comfortable with these Breathing Patterns, improvise with the Breathing Patterns to make the train your own. As all actions in the world originate on the level of thought, imagine your train as you play it.

Are you on the train? Then the sound level stays the same, although the speed may vary as it slows down or speeds up. Is it coming towards you as you wait at the station? It'll get louder and slower, until it stops! Leaving you behind at the depot? It'll speed up, and get softer, until it's so far away that you can no longer hear the clacking of the wheels — only a faint whistle, wafting back to you on the wind...

Track 13: Folk Songs, Major Scale

In this track, you'll begin learning one of the three *"Musical Alphabets"* that provide the building blocks for much of the Western World's music. But first, a bit of navigation review.

From Four to Six

Practice locating the holes 3, 4, 5, and 6, with an out breath on each. Use the very tip of your tongue to locate and count each hole up from the low end, to get a feel for the distance between them. Just aim — forget single notes.

4 5 6   4 5 6   **All Outs!**

For a real-world review, go back to page 22 and give me a round of *Taps!*

The Major Scale: A Musical Alphabet

The 26 letters of the English alphabet are used in various combinations to create words, sentences, paragraphs, and libraries full of books. The letters of the Russian alphabet produce Russian words, and long, sad Russian novels.

> *"Scales"* are musical alphabets — their notes are used as the building blocks for riffs and songs and solos. You'll learn three scales in this method. The first one is called the *"Major Scale."* It's used to play thousands of songs.
>
> If you want to play folk or classical music, make sure to practice the first six notes of this scale, right now. Of course, you'll be playing these as chords now, not single holes or notes, since we haven't gotten around to them yet!

Playing the Major Scale, Do to La

Here are the first six notes of the easiest Major Scale on the harmonica (you'll find the remaining two notes in Track 18, but you can play lots of songs with just this much). I'll write this scale out in single notes. You may be familiar with these notes by their names "do-re-mi-fa-so-la."

4	4	5	5	6	6
DO	RE	ME	FA	SO	LA

Now I'll write the same thing out as chords, since that's how I expect you to be playing it for now.

345   **345**   456   **456**   567   **567**

> Practice this Major Scale a few times right now!

Twinkle Twinkle, Piece by Piece

Spend a moment on the 4 to 6 jump. You'll actually be jumping from the 3, 4, and 5 out chord to the 5, 6, and 7 out chord. Once you've practiced this, you're ready for the first part of the song. Childish? Maybe. But a great scale exercise!

Twinkle Twinkle Little Star is composed of only three parts, each eight beats long. Here's the first, written out as single notes (but play them as chords). Practice each part along with my verbal instructions on the recording.

Twin	kle	twin	kle	lit	tle	star	(breath)
•	•	•	•	•	•	•	•
4	4	6	6	6	6	6	

Now try the second part.

How	I	won	der	what	you	are	(breath)
•	•	•	•	•	•	•	•
5	5	5	5	4	4	4	

Practice with the recording, and put the two parts together!

Twin	kle	twin	kle	lit	tle	star	(breath)
•	•	•	•	•	•	•	•
4	4	6	6	**6**	**6**	6	

How	I	won	der	what	you	are	(breath)
•	•	•	•	•	•	•	•
5	**5**	5	5	**4**	**4**	4	

Now learn the last part. In the actual song (below), you'll play it twice in the second line. So be ready to make the jump from the 4 in of the word "high" to the 6 out of the word "like.

Up	a	bove	the	world	so	high	(breath)
•	•	•	•	•	•	•	•
6	6	**5**	**5**	5	5	**4**	

Twinkle Twinkle Little Star

Now you're ready to play the whole thing! Just listen to me playing and giving vocal instructions before you try it, and don't be self-critical. As I say in my corporate psychology harmonica workshops: "Any attention paid to self-critical or negative thoughts during a task is wasted energy, as big a waste as letting air escape through your nose when you play!"

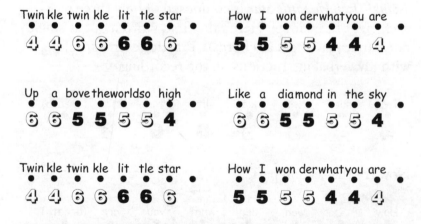

Amazing Grace

This beautiful song can be broken down into three parts as simply as *Twinkle Twinkle Little Star*. Practice each separately, then put them together. Listen to me on the recording first: I'll talk you through each part, note by note, breath by breath.

Amazing Grace Part One

A	maz	ing	grace
•	••	•	••
3	4	5	5

Amazing Grace Part Two

How	sweet	the	sound
•	••	•	••
4	4	6	6

Amazing Grace Part Three

I	once	was	lost
•	••	•	••
5	6	4	5

Put these three parts together with a few slight variations, and you've got the entire song.

You've got all the pieces, and you've already played the entire first line. The second line is almost the same as the first — just add a 4 in to 6 out to Part One. The third line combines Part Three with Part Two. And the last line begins with Part One, adds a 4 in to 4 out, then slides up on the out notes. In the notation below, I suggest some places to catch a breath.

A	maz	ing	grace	How	sweet	the	sound	(breath)
•	••	•	••	•	••	•	•	•
3	4	5	5	4	4	6	6	

To	save	a	wretch	like	me	(breath)
•	••	•	••	•	••••	•
3	4	5	5	4	6	

I	once	was	lost	but	now	am	found	(breath)
•	••	•	••	•	••	•	•	•
5	6	4	5	4	4	6	6	

Was	blind	but	now	can	see			
•	••	•	••	•	•	•	•	•
3	4	5	5	4	4	5	6	7

Track 14: Folk Songs, Minor Scale

The *"Minor Scale"* is the second of the three musical alphabets that are used to play a great deal of our so-called Western Civilization's music. The Minor Scale tends to have a more plaintive or eerie sound than the more upbeat sounding Major Scale.

Consider a monster movie. As the movie shows a carefree group of teenagers picnicking in the woods, a Major Scale based soundtrack reinforces the happy feeling of the scene. When the movie cuts to the monster lurking in the bushes, a Minor Scale based theme kicks in, to put us on edge.

In this track, I'll give you three ways to start using this scale, often associated with Eastern European, Gypsy (*Rom*), and Jewish "Klezmer" music, as well as certain types of Celtic music.

The Easiest Minor Scale

If you like, you can begin by learning the actual Minor Scale. For your information, there are two main versions, the *"Dorian Minor"* and the *"Aeolian Minor."* This is the Dorian.

4	5̄	5	6̣	6	7	7̄	8
D	E	F	G	A	B	C	D

As always, although I will write it out in single hole notation, you can aim your slightly opened mouth at the hole number I've written, and let the neighboring hole on each side play. But the Minor Scale is a bit less forgiving than the Major, so it's worth using the single note advice on page 53, then coming back and playing the Minor Scale again.

Notice that the "in-out" pattern changes to an "in-in" when you get to holes 6 and 7. Once you can play it from left to right (low to high), try it right to left (high to low).

Want more Minor Scale Songs? Go to page 81.

What Shall We Do With a Drunken Sailor?

Perhaps you'd prefer to learn the Minor Scale by playing a song — that's all right by me! This best-loved of Sea "Chanteys" or "Shanteys" is based on the Minor Scale. We could also call this a "Celtic" song, since the definition of "Celtic Music" is generally said to be "any music that comes from a place where the language Gaelic is or was spoken." Listen to my rendition on the recording, then give it a try.

What	shall	we	do	with	a	drunk	en	sai	lor
6	6	6	6	6	6	6	4	5	6

What	shall	we	do	with	a	drunk	en	sai	lor
6	6	6	6	6	6	6	4	5	6

What	shall	we	do	with	a	drunk	en	sai	lor
6	6	6	6	6	6	6	7	7	8

Ear	ly	in	the	morn	ing	
7	6	6	5	4	4	

For additional Minor Scale-based and Celtic songs (some of which are Major Scale-based), go to the "More Great Stuff" section.

"Gypsy Flamenco" Style Harmonica

The *Roma* — known to outsiders as "Gypsies" — originated in Northern India but have travelled the planet for millennia. Everywhere they go, they combine their own musical tradition with that of their host country. In Spain, the music we know as "Flamenco" was the result. The following selection provides a fine opportunity for Minor Scale improvisation.

Minor Scale Improvisation

Surprisingly, the same Breathing Patterns used for Blues and rock music will also work well for improvising Minor Scale music — with one difference. The difference? You must only use the holes 4 and higher. This forces you to use the notes of the Minor Scale, and gives you the plaintive Minor sound.

Listen to the examples of Flamenco/Gypsy-style riffs that I give you in this track, after my count of four. They're both created from the 16 beat Boogie Woogie plus Chicago Breathing Pattern (Track 11) and notated below. After these, on the recording I add some of the advanced Dirty Dog Breathing Patterns that you'll learn in Track 20.

Remember: For Minor Improv, Holes 4 through 10 only!

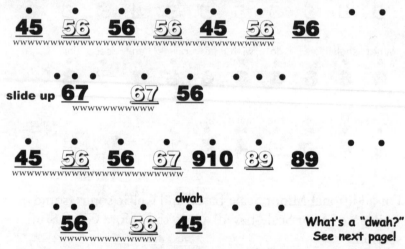

What's a "dwah?"
See next page!

Try It, and Keep On Comin' Back!

Try improvising some of your own Boogie Woogie and Chicago riffs along with me, and come back to this track for some Minor fun after you've learned more Breathing Patterns in Track 20. If you like this style of playing, read the section on playing with others, then talk a friend with a guitar, a piano, or a mandolin into playing some of these four bar, three chord verses (on page 90) for you to jamm along with!

Track 15: Dwahs and Wah-Wahs

You may have noticed that my two versions of *Amazing Grace* at the beginning and end of Track 13 were somewhat different. In the first (since I was not expecting you to play along, and wanted to show off a bit), I used *"hand wah wahs,"* two note chords instead of three, and even single notes.

The Hand Wah Wah

Since the invention of the harmonica, players have used their hands to "shape" the sound. This involves closing the space in front of the harmonica to muffle or mute it, then opening that space for a brighter, louder, sound. The pictures will help you to understand the hand position, but only many years or even decades of practice will perfect this beautiful effect.

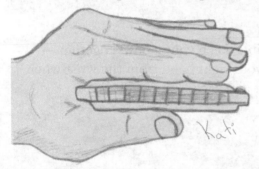

Keep your fingers lined up — no spaces between them.

The Left Handed Sandwich Grip

For the traditional wah-wah hand position, even left-handed players usually hold the harmonica in what I call the left handed sandwich hold.

Make sure that the harmonica is securely (but not painfully) pushed into the "web" of the left hand, between the thumb and forefinger. All of the fingers on top of the harp should be in a line and together — not fanned out or spread apart so that there are spaces between them.

The Right Position

The right hand is used to open and shut the air space in front of the harmonica. Most players get the best control by keeping the heels of the hands together, and the *ball* of the right thumb against the *side* of the left thumb. Try to get a good seal between the hands, but having a small open space between the hands on the side facing you is okay.

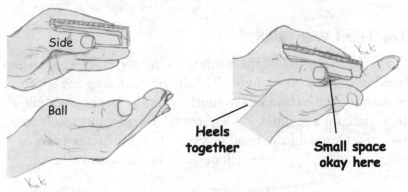

Side

Ball

Heels together

Small space okay here

Unless you are very flexible, keep your elbows together — this will help you bend your right hand from the wrist when opening and closing that air space.

On the other hand (sorry), I've seen people with the oddest hand wah-wah positions get a great sound, so experiment until you find a hand position that suits you.

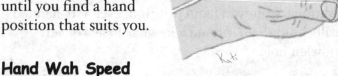

Hand Wah Speed

Hand "wahs" can be played as slowly as one wah (which is usually a closed position to open position) per beat. Or they can be played so fast that they merge into one fast, fluttering, motion (rather like the so-called Native American "war whoop," which was strictly, as I understand it, a Hollywood invention).

My Wah Demos

You can hear me, in the background, begin the song *Amazing Grace* by playing "A-maz-ing grace..." using chords with no wah-wah. Then I demonstrate some hand wah-wah tech-nique on the single notes as I play "...how sweet the sound, to save a wretch, like me-ee-ee-ee."

> A line after the word "flutter" means hold the flutter until you reach the note under the end of the line. I'll write out slower ones as wahs.

I go on to give examples of slow hand wah-wahs on single notes 4 and 3 . Then I do a more complicated wah riff. Try it yourself, but vary the timing to make it your own...

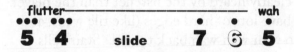

In my demonstration of the Chicago riff, I do three single wahs on the long in, then a "flutter" on the out and last in (which I hold longer than usual).

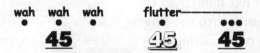

> The key to a good hand wah-wah is to make sure than your hands block as much of the air as possible when in closed position, and block no air at all when open. Since everyone has different sized hands, everyone has a slightly different hand wah-wah position.

Wah-Wah Hints

Do at least some wah-wah practice in the bathroom, for three reasons. Firstly, the mirror will show you if your right hand is completely blocking the air, or if you are leaving "gaps." As I wrote and illustrated on page 50, a small space on the side *facing* you is okay.

But on the *back side?* Closed means closed — you don't want to see hands like these in the mirror! Get a good seal between those hands!

This is why we check our hand Wah-Wah in the mirror!

Kati

Secondly, the wah-wah sound projects outwards, away from you — it is more clearly heard by the listener than the player. Most bathrooms have lots of hard edges (like tile walls, and mirrors) that echo your wah-wah back to you. Stairwells and pedestrian tunnels are also good for wah-ing, and for playing in general — nice acoustics!

An Exercise That's All Wet

Lastly, here's a great hand wah-wah exercise. Put the fingers of your left hand over the fingers of your right hand, with the fingers at right angles to each other. Bring the heels of your hands together. This is the classic "use your hands to cup some water" position. It's also quite close to the ideal hand wah-wah position — if your hands will hold water, you've got a good seal between them. So cup a handful of water, and try to keep it from leaking out for as long as possible!

Kati

Single Notes

If you haven't already experimented with getting the two hole chords described on page 34 in Track Ten, you'd probably better put in a few minutes on them right now. If you have, you're ready to start working on your single notes.

Actually, you may already have played a single note on the 1 hole, back in Track 11 on page 36. But the technique involved in getting any of the higher single notes is completely different.

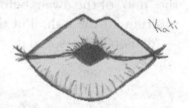

To play a single note, you'll have to pucker your lips as though you were whistling, then push the harmonica slightly in between them.

As always, the harmonica must be well under the upper lip and over the lower, or the flesh of your lips will block part of the hole, and give you a choked or muffled sound.

On the Tip of Your Tongue

During practice, use the tip of your tongue to locate the center of the hole that you're aiming at (of course, you can't do this while trying to play a song.)

Don't worry if getting single notes is hard to do at first — it is — but there is nothing in this book that absolutely requires them. Just keep working on two hole chords (which will strengthen your pucker muscle, or *orbicularis oris*), and spend a few minutes a day trying to play using single notes.

The "Dwah" Effect

Say the word "dwah" (of course it's a word, at least for harp players). Now say it slowly, almost as a "doo-wah." Think about the motion of your tongue — it probably starts out touching the roof of your mouth just behind your front teeth, to prepare for the "duh" or d' sound of the dwah.

Air pressure builds up behind the tongue, and it tenses. Then, like a dam bursting, it drops down and back, to form the "doo" of the dwah, before returning to a normal, relaxed, position for the wah. Put the three parts together smoothly — "duh-oo-ah" — speed it up, and there's your dwah.

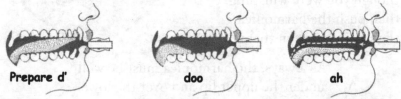

Prepare d'   doo   ah

While keeping your lips in single note or two note chord position (this is important, so don't let them open up on the "wah" of the dwah!), practice saying some dwahs. Now — and here's the tricky part — do it on the inhale!

Listen to my examples. Start empty. Keep your nose closed. Don't let your lips separate at all when you get to the "ah" part. Just make the exact same dwah tongue motion as you do on the out breath. Like everything else, it will feel strange at first but come with practice. Dwahs are most commonly used on the two hole chords 3 and 4, 4 and 5, and 5 and 6.

Dwah-ing the Boogie Woogie

Throw a dwah on each of the in breaths for more interesting Boogie Woogie riffs. Here's my first of two examples.

dwah   •   dwah   •   dwah   •   dwah   •   •
45   <u>45</u>   **34**   <u>45</u>   **45**   <u>45</u>   **34**

And here's my second example.

dwah		dwah		dwah		dwah		
•	•	•	•	•	•	•	•	•
45	**45**	**34**	**45**	**56**	**56**	**45**		

Dwah the Dirty Dogs

Dwahs also add some bite to your Dirty Dog riffs, as in my examples. When doing a series of dwahs in swing beat, I often alternate each dwahs with a da — it helps to swing the beat, since the da is faster to say than the dwah (and in a swing the first part of the beat lasts longer than the second, as you no doubt recall).

dwah	da	dwah	da	dwah	
•		•		•	•
45	**45**	**45**	**45**	**45**	(silent beat)

dwah	da	dwah	da	dwah	
•		•		•	•
45	**45**	**56**	**56**	**67**	

Add some dwahs to your riffs — a good dwah on the last in note (before the three beat silence) of a Chicago Breathing Pattern works very well indeed! If you look back to page 48, you'll see that I combined a shake with a dwah on my last Chicago riff during the Gypsy/Flamenco Jamm. And you'll use some dwahs in the rock and roll bridge on the next track.

> I'm sorry to keep "harping" on the subject. But I cannot emphasize enough that this method relies heavily on listening and doing. So if you tend to be primarily a reader, please remember to spend some time with the recording, as well...

Track 16: Some Easy Hard Rock

By the time you finish this track, you'll be able to play a
Twelve Bar rock and roll solo similar to the one in my intro,
including a rock and roll "bridge."

The Rock and Roll Bridge

A "bridge" is a piece of music that comes in between two
pieces of music that are similar to each other. It's often the
most dramatic (and loudest) part of a music verse. In this
case, we'll use a bridge to connect two of my favorite rock
and roll Breathing Patterns. I'll write this eight beat, two bar
bridge down with dwahs, but you can vary it by using one wah
per beat, or a flutter wah — or all of the above!

Try dwahs and flutters at the same time!

dwah	dwah	dwah	dwah	•	• • •
•	•	•	•		
45	**45**	**45**	**45**	**45**	**(3 silent beats)**

Dave's Favorite Rock Breathing Pattern

Memorize this two bar breathing pattern, starting with
practice in the middle of the harmonica. Use some dahs on
the in breaths, to make them nice and clear. But emphasize
the out breaths — make them crisp and forceful — to give
this Breathing Pattern a real rock and roll feel, since rock and
roll usually emphasizes the second and fourth beat of every bar.
Try it first on a two (or three) hole chord in the middle.

Don't forget the two beats of silence at the end of the pattern!

in in out in in out in in out in • •

45 45 45 45 45 45 45 45 45 45

Five Rock Riff Demos

Once you own this Breathing Pattern, apply it in a variety of places, along with my verbal instructions. In my examples I'll start you on the 1, 2, and 3 hole chord — keep it wide and open to avoid the choked sound.

123 123 123 123 123 123 123123 123 123 ··

Then you'll start moving it around. I'll mostly notate these as two note chords, but use three if you need to, and don't worry about the exact notes, except when you end on the 1 in. Watch those silent beats!

Low to High Rock Riff

23 23 34 34 34 56 567 567 678 910 ··

High to Way Low Rock Riff (a cool ending for a verse)

910 910 89 45 45 45 23 23 23 1 ··

Jump Outs to the Middle Rock Riff (in slide down to the last low in)

23 23 45 23 23 45 23 23 45 12 ··

34 Dwah Rock Riff

dwah dwah   dwah dwah   dwah dwah   dwah
34 34 45 34 34 45 34 34 45 34 ··

Don't Get Discouraged — This Took Me Four Years!

Now apply this pattern *anywhere* you like, shaking and sliding, wahing and dwahing. Make it crisp, and don't forget the silences! Don't get discouraged if some of these seem hard — as I said, I was playing for four years before I could do this well (and how long have you been playing so far?).

Twelve Bar Rock & Roll Solos: A Recipe for Success

Our Rock Breathing Pattern and the Bridge are both two
bars long. So we can easily improvise a Twelve Bar rock solo
by combining six of them. This is the order to do it in:

Four Rock Breathing Patterns

One Rock Bridge

One Last Rock Breathing Pattern (often high to very low)

You can use any notes or special effects that you like on the
Rock Breathing Patterns, and this *"recipe"* for a Twelve Bar
rock solo will always work!

The First Demo Rock Verse

The first of my two examples is very simple, although it
sounds great. You can see how both of these verses fit the
Twelve Bar rock solo recipe.

123 123 123 123 123 123 123123 123 123 ••

123 123 123 123 123 123 123123 123 123 ••

45 45 45 45 45 45 45 45 45 45 ••

123 123 123 123 123 123 123123 123 123 ••

Flutter
•• ••   •   • • •
**Get empty for
the Bridge!**   **45   45**

123 123 123 123 123 123 123123 123 123 ••

As I've mentioned before — the notation for the following rock solo, as well as the one on the previous page, *looks* complicated. Playing the actual solos while listening to my verbal instruction is far easier, since they're both based on simple Breathing Patterns...

The Second Demo Rock Verse

23 23 45 23 23 45 23 23 45 23

23 23 45 23 23 45 23 23 45 23

dwah dwah   dwah dwah   dwah dwah   dwah
45 45 45 34 34 45 45 45 45 34

23 23 45 45 45 56 56 56 56 45

dwah dwah dwah dwah
Get empty for
the Bridge!   **45 45 45 45 45**

89 89 56 45 45 45 23 23 23 1

That's rockin'! And now might be a good time to go to Playalong Track 22 — The Classic Rock Playalong — and make up some solos of your own.

Track 17: The Rhymin' Blues

In my humble opinion, the master skill — the most important ability that a human being can attain — is the ability to control one's own mind and emotions. As I discuss in the recording, the *"Dozens,"* or Rhyming Blues, is a prime example of this. To me the very genesis of the blues was an attempt to achieve mental mastery by turning angst into art — transforming the pain of slavery and second-class citizenship into some of the most creative forms of music that the world has ever known.

The Rhymin' Blues Riff

This riff and its variations form the basis of a thousand songs, by Janis Joplin and J. Geils, by every Blues and most rock players. Practice the Breathing Pattern on the middle holes first. Make sure you don't play during the silent beats — they're reserved for your lyrics! Start after the count of three:

in   **out**   **in**   **in**   (two silent beats)

456   **456**   **456**   **456**   (two silent beats)

Simplified Timing

If the timing of this seems difficult, we can triple the beat until you get the hang of it, as in the following line. Once you do, keep playing, but look at the line above this one, and only tap your foot four times instead of twelve.

in   **out**   **in**   **in**   (seven silent beats)

456   **456**   **456**   **456**   (seven silent beats)

If you continue to have any problems with the timing of this riff, listen — lots — to my recorded examples.

The Low Down Rhymin' Blues Riff

If you've worked at getting good tone from your low end notes, try it down there — nice and low and mellow.

123   **123**   **123**   **123** **(two silent beats)**

Or with simplified timing:

123   **123**   **123**   **123**   • • • • • • • **(seven silent beats)**

The Real Rhymin' Blues Riff

After you've mastered the Rhymin' Blues Riff on the middle and low holes, try taking it where it belongs, with a dwah aimed at the 3, or the 3 and 4 holes.

123   **345**   _dwah_ **34**   **123** **(two silent beats)**

Or with simplified timing:

123   **345**   _dwah_ **34**   **123**   • • • • • • • **(seven silent beats)**

You might even want to try it with single notes:

2   **4**   _dwah_ **3**   **2** **(two silent beats)**

Finish it Off with a...Shake!

I like to end this type of song with a shake on the 4 and 5 in.

Fancier Variations of the Rhymin' Blues Riff

There are many. For example, an extra 4 in or 345 in can be added, for a slightly different Rhymin' Riff (the first one I demonstrate when discussing the variations) similar to that used in my *Bad Olympics* intro and the song *Bad to the Bone,* by George Thorogood (and lately a rap favorite).

123 345 345 34 123 (two silent beats)

Or, with simplified timing, single notes, and my intro lyrics:

2 4 4 3 2 You're the bad- dest of bad

Ready-Made Blues/Rap Style Songs

You can flatter your friends or dis your enemies, entertain your co-workers, and leave the world's greatest answering machine messages — just by inserting a name into these ready-made rhymin' Blues. To keep the beat right, you may need to "adjust" the number of syllables in the name, so a David might become a Dave, and a Jennifer might need to be a Jen.

You can use the simplest middle hole two beat version, or the fanciest. I'll write the 2 in-4 out-4 in- 3 in-2 in riff in the parentheses, but you can put whichever riff you like into the two beats of riff that alternate with the lyrics. Just remember, when singing, that the syllable under the dot gets emphasized, the other syllables fall in between the beats.

On the next page you'll find a slight variation on the song I use during the intro to this track. You can use it yourself as a "fill-in-the-blanks" song that can be either a roast or a toast, depending on how the listener interprets the word "bad." Listen to my Rhymin' Blues on the recording for help with the timing, then play it for a pal!

The Bad Olympics: A Fill-in-the-Blanks Rhymin' Blues

(2 4 4 3 2) (*Dave's*) the bad- dest of bad

(2 4 4 3 2) You just lis- ten to me

(2 4 4 3 2) 'cause (*his/her*) mid- dle name

(2 4 4 3 2) Is spell'd B- A- D

(2 4 4 3 2) Be- cause (*s)he's* so Ba- ad

(2 4 4 3 2) If the truth must be told

(2 4 4 3 2) At the Baaad O- lym- pics

(2 4 4 3 2) (*S)he'd* go home with the go-old (45 shake)

A Love or Friendship Rhymin' Blues (not on recording)

(2 4 3 2) You know when I'm hav- in'

(2 4 3 2) A mis- ra- ble day

(2 4 3 2) The sound of (*Kate's*) voice

(2 4 3 2) Blows my Blues far a-way (45 shake)

To create a song of your own, think of two rhyming words and the idea that connects them. Then create a four line "poem," in which lines two and four rhyme. Throw your riff in before each line, end with a 45 shake, and you've got it!

Track 18: More Folk Songs, and Playing By Ear

The key (if you'll pardon the pun) to playing by ear is to know the Major Scale — backwards and forwards, up and down — until you can play it in your sleep! So you'll begin this track by learning to play the full Major Scale, with the two notes that we've left out so far.

The Full Major Scale

Here it is. The shift in Breathing Pattern from out-in on holes 4, 5, and 6 to in-out on 7 will fool you, at first. Play it both from low to high, and high to low. I'll write this out in single notes, but just aim and play chords if you can't go single!

4	4	5	5	6	6	7	7
C	D	E	F	G	A	B	C
do	re	mi	fa	so	la	ti	do

I've also included the letter names of these notes (as played on our key of C harmonicas, as well as the "solfege" (do-re-mi) names. Since this Major Scale starts on a "C" note, it's called a *"C Major Scale,"* or a *"Major Scale in the key of C."* If you're interested in why music works as it does, read about my book *Music Theory Made Easy* in the "Where to Go from Here" section.

The Case of the Missing Notes

In order to make all the notes of the harmonica, well, harmonious — two notes of the Major Scale were omitted from the low end, and one from the high end. (If you want the full details, you'll find them in my *Music Theory Made Easy for Harmonica*). On the next page is a diagram that shows this. Notice the lack of an F and an A note in the low end, and the lack of a B note in the high end.

The ABC's of the Harmonica

Hole #:	1	2	3	4	5	6	7	8	9	10
Out notes:	C	E	G	C	E	G	C	E	G	C
In notes:	D	G	B	D	F	A	B	D	F	A

We've already learned to compensate for this. When playing *Amazing Grace,* it would be nice *not* to have to make those 4 in to 6 in jumps. But try playing it using the low end:

A	maz	ing	grace	How	sweet	the	sound
●	●●	●	●●	●	●●	●	●●
3	4	5	5	4	4	X	3

Unless you can "bend" notes, an advanced technique used mostly by Blues players, it can't be done. The note for "the" — an "A" note — is not there for you in the low end, although it's perfectly accessible up at 6 in. Pretty much anytime you see a song of mine with a 4 in to 6 in jump — like *Amazing Grace, Danny Boy, Red River Valley,* or many others — the jump is there to avoid a missing note in the low end.

The Jumping Major Scale

Some songs need to start on the note 4 out and head down, Practicing this scale will eliminate the "Where the heck is that note?" problem that plagues most beginning harmonica players — and discourages many from continuing. Play it with chords or single notes — it'll work fine either way

4	3	6	6	5	5	4	4
C	B	A	G	F	E	D	C

Following are two great songs that will hone your real life Major Scale skills!

Oh When the Saints

In the intro to this track, I threw a few extra flourishes (like the ending, in parentheses) into this great Dixieland tune, mostly during the long notes and silences at the end of lines. It can be played slow or fast. In fact, in New Orleans it's often used at funerals, played slowly on the way to the cemetery to mourn the deceased, and fast on the way back, to celebrate his or her life!

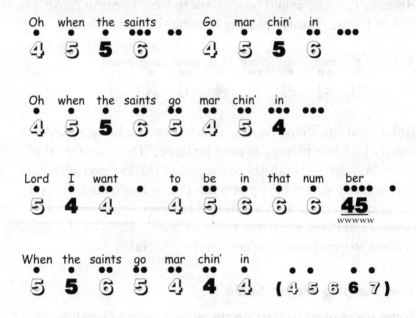

If the ending (in parens) seems a bit much, just hold the last 4 out note for five beats, fading it towards the end...

Beethoven's Ninth, The Ode to Joy

Much classical music is based on the Major Scale, although the Minor Scale is also used. In fact, lots of classical music is actually based on earlier folk tunes, so the line between folk and classical music is blurred, as is the line between Blues and rock. You can hear the first two lines of this most-loved Fourth Movement of *Beethoven's Ninth Symphony* at the end of this track.

The Fourth Movement of the Ninth Symphony

5 5 6 6 5 5 4

4 4 4 5 5 4 4

5 5 5 6 6 5 5

4 4 4 4 5 4 4

4 5 4 4 5 5 5

4 4 5 5 5 4 4 4 3

5 5 6 6 5 5 4

4 4 4 5 4 4 4

Figuring Out Songs "by Ear"

If you know what scale a song is based on and the first note or notes, it's usually easy to figure out the rest. On the next page are the first lines of a few songs. Choose one and see if you can find the rest of the notes, one at a time. You may want to write each note down (4 out-3 in etc.) as you locate them by trial and error. Just ask yourself: "Should the next note sound higher, lower, or the same?" Then try it — if that note doesn't work — try another! As many songs have repeated sections, it goes faster than you'd expect!

Figuring Out a Song by Ear, From the First Line

Choose one of these songs that you know well.

These songs are all based on the Major Scale, so play it (page 64) a few times before looking for the notes of the rest of the song.

And if you absolutely can't find a note that seems like it should be lower than 4 out, it is most probably a missing note, so try jumping up to the 6 in, or less likely, the 5 in.

For example, try to figure out the first song below. When you come to the notes for the "Oh Su- zan- nah" part — you'll need to use a double 5 in then a double 6 in (unless you're already good at "bending" notes, which is unlikely). The "sleigh" in the "Dashing through the snow..." part of *Jingle Bells* will require a 6 in jump, also.

Oh	I	went	to	Al	a	ba	ma	with	my	ban	jo	on	my	knee
4	**4**	5	6	6	**6**	6	5	4	**4**	5	5	**4**	4	**4**

I	come	on		the	Sloop	John	B.		My	gran	fa	ther	an	me
3	5	5		5	5	**5**	5		3	5	5	5	**5**	5

Frer	e	Jac	que		Frer	e	Jac	que		Dor	mez	vous?		Dor	mez	vous
4	**4**	5	4		4	**4**	5	4		5	**5**	6		5	**5**	6

Fran	kie	and	John	nie	were	lo	vers		Lor	dy	but	how	they	did	love
4	5	6	**6**	6	5	4	4		4	5	6	**6**	6	5	4

Jin	gle	bells		jin	gle	bells		jin	gle	all	the	way		oh	what	fun
5	5	5		5	5	5		5	6	4	**4**	5		**5**	**5**	**5**

Mi	chael	row	the	boat	a	shore		Hal	le	liu	yah		Mich	ael	row	the
4	5	6	5	6	**6**	6		5	6	**6**	6		5	6	6	5

From the First Note Alone...

If you know just the first note of a song, it's harder but not too hard to figure out the rest. All of the following are Major Scale-based, so play that a few times before you try each song. These songs are all copyrighted, so I can't give you the entire song. But if you like these great artists (Mr. Dylan was my first harmonica inspiration and idol — I bought my first harp as a fashion accessory, to look like my hero), buy their recordings, and attend their concerts!

Bob Dylan's *Blowin' In the Wind* starts on a 6 out.

His *Hey Mr. Tambourine Man* begins with a 7 out.

Peter, Paul, & Mary's *Puff the Magic Dragon* starts on 7 out.

Billy Joel's *Piano Man* starts on 6 out.

In the Jungle (Weem-o-Wep, The Lion Sleeps Tonight) starts on 4 out.

The great show tune *Oklahoma* starts on 7 out.

If I Only Had a Brain jumps a lot, and starts on 5 out.

Do, A Deer from *The Sound of Music* starts on a do note, 4 out, of course. It has one note that will have to be "fudged" — it requires a bend on the word "that" in the last line, but 6 in will be an "okay" substitute note. It's a great way to practice the Major Scale!

No Notes to Start With...

If you don't even have the first note, but suspect that the song is based on the Major Scale, try this: play (yes, again) the Major Scale a few times. If the song starts higher and works its way down in the first few notes, try starting with a 6 out or 7 out. If it starts lower and works its way up, try 4 out, then 3 out, then 5 out. It's unusual for a Major Scale-based song to start on an in note, but it could happen. So if none of the above works, try some ins! Good luck!

Track 19: Putting it All Together

There's not really too much to say about this track, except: *Congratulations!* If you've made it this far, you can play more than I could after years of teaching myself. Luckily, I'm a better harp teacher now! Where was I, back when I needed me?

A Playalong Hint

Spend lots of time with the Playalong Tracks. Use the Breathing Patterns that you know before learning the new ones in Track 20. Play what you play with zest and feeling, even if you can't play much.

Ideas for Other Breathing Pattern Combinations

Put the Breathing Patterns together in different ways — either with or without the playalong music. Maybe a train rhythm would fit just fine in between a Boogie Woogie and a Chicago Pattern. Try using a bar of inhaled Dirty Dogs then a bar of exhaled Dirty Dogs to replace the Rock Bridge in a solo.

Combine a Boogie Woogie Pattern with a Rock Bridge. Or try a Rock Bridge variation, by fitting a bar of the new Dirty Dogs from Track 20 (without the last silent beat) into the Bridge's three beats of silence (in-in-in-in-out-Dirty Dirty Dog). Try the same with the Chicago Riff — add a set of Track 20's Dirty Dogs, *sans* silent beat (innnn-out-in-Dirty-Dirty-Dog). Try anything — be creative in putting together what you know!

Forget and Forgive, Once in a While

Once in a while, forget everything you know and just blow! Promise yourself, in advance, that you're going to make mistakes and just keep going. If you do this with the Playalong Tracks, keep just one thing in mind — when in doubt, inhale. Inhaling anywhere will always fit in when playing Blues or rock, if you put feeling and rhythm into it!

Track 20: A Few More BP's

If you can use the Chicago and Boogie Woogie Breathing Patterns with confidence, you're ready to vary them!

Boogie Woogie Variations

Simply by changing the timing of our standard Boogie Woogie Breathing Pattern — lengthening some breaths, and shortening others — we create more interesting variations.

Here are three of my favorites, with a new timing notation. If you see half a dot above a note, play it for half a beat. See one and a half dots above a note? Play it for one and a half beats. Listen to these examples on the recording, to get the beat.

Boogie Woogie Breathing Pattern Variation Number One

in out in out in out in

45 45 45 45 45 45 45

dwah

34 45 45 56 56 56 45

Boogie Woogie Breathing Pattern Variation Number Two

in out in out in out in

45 45 45 45 45 45 45

dwah　　　　　　**dwah**　　**dwah**

34 45 45 45 34 45 45

Boogie Woogie Breathing Pattern Variation Number Three

in out **in** out in **out** **in** •

45 45 **45** 45 **45** 45 **45**

56 56 **45** 45 **34** 45 **45**
wwwww   wwww   wwwwwwwwww

This one has lots of half beats and one and a halves. Make up some Boogie Woogie timing variations of your own, too.

Dirty Dirty Dog Variations

Now we come to the "real" use of the Dirty Dog rhythm. Instead of using all inhales or all exhales, you'll use the basic rhythm as a Breathing Pattern. Here's the most basic one — a single bar long. Naturally, you can move it around and add effects like shakes, slides, wahs and dwahs.

dirrr	d'	dirrr	d'	dog	
in	out	**in**	out	**in**	(silent)
45	45	**45**	45	**45**	•

My first two examples use only the 4 and 5 holes (above). I'll write the fancier third and fourth ones out for you, below.

		dwah		dwah	
slide up	67	**45**	45	**34**	•

dwah		dwah		dwah	
34	45	**45**	45	**34**	•

The Chicago Dog

Take the first two beats of the previous Breathing Pattern, and substitute them for the first two beats of the Chicago Breathing Pattern. Don't forget the three silent beats!

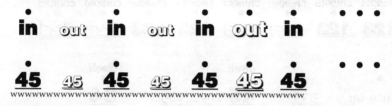

in out **in** out **in** out **in** • • •

45 45 **45** 45 **45** 45 **45** • • •
wwwwwwwwwwwwwwwwwwwwwwwwwwwwwwwwwwwwwwwwww

My first example of this, above, uses only the two hole chord on 4 and 5, with lots of shaking. My second is fancier:

dwah

slide 67 **56** 56 **45** 45 **34** • • •

Another Great 16 Beat Breathing Pattern

Take two of the new one bar Dirty Dog Patterns, and add one of the new two bar Chicago Dog Patterns — you'll produce a four bar Breathing Pattern that can be used to create limitless numbers of fine riffs. Here's my example, but make up lots of your own, with slides, shakes, wahs, dwahs — whatever you can think of (or do without thinking). Notice how I combine dwahs and single wahs (wah/dwah) and shakes in the same riff.

wah/dwah   wah/dwah   wah/dwah

34 45 **45** 45 **34**   •

wah/dwah   wah/dwah   wah/dwah

34 45 **45** 45 **34** slide down

wah/dwah   dwah   dwah   dwah

34 45 **45** 45 **34** 45 **34** • • •
wwwwwwwwwwwwwwwwwwwwwwwwwwwwwwwww

In Articulation Training

When you can add "chukkas" on each in and out breath of the train, you know that your articulation is in good shape! And why not try a Dirty Dog Whistle, for a change?

chukka	chukka	chukka	chukka	chukka	chukka	chukka	chukka
123	123	123	123	123	123	123	123

		dwah			dwah	
slide up	67	45	45	34	

		dwah			dwah	
slide up	67	45	45	34	

chukka	chukka	chukka	chukka	chukka	chukka	chukka	chukka
123	123	123	123	123	123	123	123

Train's Gone!

Heavy Rock Boogie Riff

If you like the Rock Boogie in Track 10 and Playalong Track 23, you can learn to play a version of it on the harmonica, as you can hear me doing at the beginning of Playalong Track 23. Here are three successively harder versions — keep a steady and swingin' beat and play 'em over and over.

da	da	dwah		da	da	dwah	
2	2	3	4	2	2	3	4

da	da	d'	dwah		da	da	d'	dwah	
2	2	2	3	4	2	2	2	3	4

da	da	d'	dwah		da	da	d'	dwah	
2	2	2	3	4	432 in slide	2	2	2	3	4	432 in slide

Track 21: Guitar Blues Playalong

A single guitar player makes a great accompaniment for a harp player, as you'll see from this medium speed guitar Boogie Woogie! Any of your Breathing Patterns will work with this track. The two harmonica solos at the end are used to demonstrate Blues Scales, and are notated on pages 85 and 86.

Track 22: Classic Rock Playalong

The band gets down here, especially the drummer! Use the Rock Solo Recipe from page 58 to create your own verses, or use any of the Breathing Patterns you know to play riffs that'll go with this rockin' background music.

The last verse demonstrates how an advanced beginner would add to the Rock Breathing Pattern from Track 16. If this appeals to you, check out my *Instant Blues Harmonica* — it features more info on improvising strategy using this type of riff.

Track 23: Blues Rock Boogie

You're welcome to join me in playing the Rock Boogie Riffs from page 74, or you can use any of the Breathing Patterns to play along. If you need inspiration, the ends of both Tracks 10 and 11 (pages 34 and 37) will help.

In general, all of the Breathing Patterns you've learned can be used with these tracks. Review Track 19 for some playalong hints, and learn the additional Breathing Patterns in Track 20 — when you feel ready. Now playalong, and enjoy!

Note: CD users can skip back and use the playalongs at the end of Track 9 (Dirty Dogs Two Chord Rock) and Track 14 (Gypsy/Flamenco Minor Jamm).

More Great Stuff

Here I offer you some information I wanted to include but that either didn't seem to need to be on the recording, or didn't seem to fit in elsewhere. Country Music, extra Major and Minor songs, a little more of the music theory underlying the Blues, a description of the "bending" technique, and Jamm Session Etiquette. Just look at the headings, then decide what you want to read now and what you want to leave for later...

Country Music

To me, country music falls into two general categories: "Cowboy" songs, and C & W improvisation. There's a great scale for improvising Country and Western music, but it is beyond the scope of this book. (But if that's your interest, check out my *C & W Harmonica Made Easy*.) Here, I'd just like to give you a few of my Cowboy favorites. Like most country songs, these are based on the Major Scale.

Red River Valley   (notice the jump to avoid a low missing note)

From	this	val	ley	they	say	you	are	go	ing	
3	4	5	5	4	4	4	5	4	4	

We	will	miss	your	bright	eyes	and	sweet	smile	
3	4	5	4	5	6	5	5	4	

On	this	day	you	are	tak	ing	the	sun	shine	
6	5	5	5	4	4	4	5	6	5	

That	had	bright	ened	our	path	for	a	while
6	6	6	3	4	4	5	4	4

Oh Shenandoah

Oh	Shen	an	doah	I	long	to	hear	you
3	4	4	4	4	5	5	6	6

Far	a	way	you	roll	ing	ri	ver
7	7	6	6	6	6	5	6

Oh	Shen	an	doah	I	long	to	hear	you
6	6	6	6	5	6	5	4	4

A	way		I'm	gone	a	way	
3	4	.	4	5	6	6	.

'cross	the	wide	Mis	sour	ri	
4	4	5	4	4	4	.

Home on the Range   (also jumps to avoid a low missing note)

Oh	give	me	a	home		where	the	buf-	fa-	lo	roam
7	6	7	8	8	.	7	7	6	5	5	5

and	the	deer	and	the	an-	te-	lope	play	
5	5	6	4	4	4	3	4	4	.

And	sel-	dom	is	heard		a	dis-	cour-	a-	ging	word
3	3	4	4	5	.	7	7	6	5	5	5

and	the	skies	are	not	cloud-	y	all	day	
5	5	5	4	4	3	4	4	4	.

More Major Scale Songs

These will be easy to play if you've practiced the Major Scale in Track 18. Don't worry about getting single notes — just aim your lips at the right hole and keep track of your ins and outs.

My Country 'tis of Thee/God Save the Queen

4 4 **4** 3 4 4   5 5 **5** 5 4 4

4 4 3 4

Outlined Numbers = Breathe Out!
"Filled In" Numbers = Breath In!

6 6 6 6 **5** 5   **5** **5** **5** 5 5 4

5 **5** 5 4 4 5 5 6 6 5 5 4 4

On Top of Old Smoky

On	top	of	old	Smo	ky		all	cov	er'd	with	snow
4	4	5	6	7	**6**		**6**	5	6	6	6

I	lost	my	true	lov	er		a	court	in'	too	slow
4	4	5	6	6	**4**		5	**5**	5	4	4

Morning Has Broken

Morn	ing	has	bro	ken	like	the	first	mor	ning
4	5	6	7	**8**	7	6	6	6	6

Black	bird	is	sing	ing	like	the	first	bird		
4	**4**	5	6	6	6	5	4	**4**	6	6

Praise for his sing ing
6 5 6 7 6

Praise for the mor ning
6 5 4 4 4

Praise for them spring ing
5 4 5 6 6

fresh from the word
4 5 4 4

Blow the Man Down

Now all you young sai lors that fol low the sea
5 6 6 6 5 4 5 6 6 6 5

With a Yo! Ho! Blow the man down!
4 5 6 6 5 5 5 4

Now please pay at ten tion and lis ten to me
3 4 5 4 3 2 3 4 5 4 3

And give me a chance to blow the man down!
4 6 6 6 6 5 5 4 5 4

Brahms Lullaby

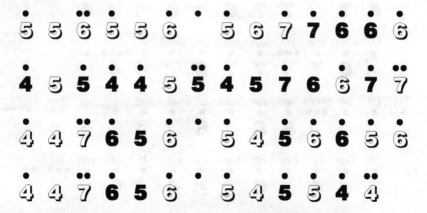

5 5 6 5 5 6 5 6 7 7 6 6 6

4 5 5 4 4 5 5 4 5 7 6 6 7 7

4 4 7 6 5 6 5 4 5 6 6 5 6

4 4 7 6 5 6 5 4 5 5 4 4

Good Morning to You (Melody of "The Birthday Song")

A good mor- ning to you   A good mor- ning to you
6 6 **6** 6 **7** **7**   6 6 **6** 6 **8** 7

A good mor- ning dear sis- ter   A good mor- ning to you
6 6 **9** 8 7 **7** 6   **5** **5** **5** 4 **4** **4**

Oh Danny Boy

Oh Dan ny boy   the Ker ry pipes are ca all ing
3 4 **4** 5   **4** 5 **6** 6 5 4 **4** **6**

from glen to glen   and down the moun tain side
3 4 **4** 5   **6** 6 5 4 5 **4**

The sum mer's gone   and all the flow'rs are dy yy ing
3 4 **4** 5   **4** 5 **6** 6 5 4 **4** **6**

'Tis you 'tis you must go 'tis I 'tis I must bide
3 4 **4** 5 **6** 6 5 **4** 4 **6** **7** 7

But come ye back when sum mers in the mea ea ea dow
6 **6** **7** 7 **7** 7 6 6 6 5 4 **4**

Or when the val leys hush'd and white wi' snow
6 **6** **7** 7 **7** 7 6 6 5 **4**

'Tis I'll be there in sun light or in sha a a dow
6 6 6 8 **8** **8** 7 **6** 7 6 5 4 **4**

Oh Dan ny boy oh Dan ny boy I love you so
3 4 **4** 5 **6** 6 5 **4** 4 **6** **7** 7

More Minor Scale Songs

These songs are all based on the Dorian Minor Scale of Track 14 (on page 46 — practice it if you find these difficult). As with the Major Scale, many of these songs require "jumps" to avoid missing low notes. Use your wahs, shakes, and dwahs!

Good Mornin' Blues

This is a Twelve Bar Minor Blues: its chord structure is on page 91. The Twelve Bar should start when you hit the word "mor."

Good	mor	nin'	Blu	ues		Blues	how	do	you	do		
4	**6**	⑥	**5**	**4**		**6**	⑥	**5**	**4**	**45**	**45**	**45**

Good	mor	nin'	Blu	ues		Blues	how	do	you	do		
4	**6**	⑥	**5**	**4**		**6**	⑥	**5**	**4**	**45**	**45**	**45**

I'm	feel'n	al	right	good	mor	ning	how	are	you		
5	⑤	⑤	⑤	⑤	**5**	⑤	**4**	**4**	**45**	**45**	**45**

House of the Rising Sun

There	is	a	house	in	New	Or-	leans	
6	**4**	**4**	**5**	**6**	⑥	**4**	**5**	

	they	call	the	ris-	in'	sun	
	⑥	**6**	⑦	⑥	⑥	**6**	

And	it's	been	the	ruin	of	this	poor	boy	
6	⑦	**8**	**8**	⑦	**6**	⑥	**4**	**5**	

He's	not	the	on-	-	ly	one	No!	
5	**4**	**5**	⑤	**5**	⑤	**45** slide	**6**	

Saint James Infirm'ry

Went	down	to	Saint	James	In	firm	ry	
6	6	5	6	6	6	5	45	

Saw	my	ba-	by	was	a	ly	ing	there	
5	6	6	6	6	6	8	8	6	

Laid	out	on	a	sur-	ge-	ry	ta-	ble	
67	67	67	5	6	6	6	5	4	

So	cold	so	white	so	pa-	le	so	fair	
4	5	4	5	67	67	67	56	45	

Scarborough Fair (Parsley Sage Rosemary & Thyme)

Are	you	go-	ing	to	Scar-	bor-	ough	fair	
4	4	6	6	5	5	5	5	4	

Par-	sley	sage	rose-	mar-	y	and	thyme	
6	7	8	7	6	7	6	6	

Re-	mem-	ber	me	to	one	who	lives	the-	er-	e	
4	4	4	4	6	6	6	5	5	4	4	

She	once	was	a	true	love	of	mine
4	6	6	5	5	4	4	4

5	5	6	5	5	5	5	4	4

Minor Scale Songs — The Missing Notes

If you practice the Minor Scale on page 46, and this new "jumping" variation to avoid the low end missing notes, you'll be able to play many Minor Scale based songs, although you may have to "fudge" a note, as in "la-a-dy" *Greensleeves!*

Jumping Minor: 4 4 3 6 6 5 5 4

Greensleeves

A	las	my	lo	ove	you	do	me	wro	ong	to
4	5	6	6	7	6	6	5	4	4	5

cast	me	ou	ut	dis	cour	teous	ly
5	4	4	4	4	5	4	6

For	I	do	love	you	with	all	my	he	art
4	5	6	6	7	6	6	5	4	4

and	who	but	my	la	a	dy	Greensleeves		
5	5	5	4	4	6	7 slide	4	4

Green	sle	eves	was	all	my	joy
7	7	7	6	6	5	4

Green	sle	eves	was	my	de	light
5	5	5	4	5	4	6

Greensleeves	was	my	heart	of	go	old
7	7	7	6	6	5	4	4

and	who	but	my	la	a	dy	Greensleeves	
5	5	5	4	4	6	7 slide	4	4

> Gershwin's Summertime, My favorite Minor song, starts on the 6 in and jumps there any time a note is missing...

The Blues Scale

The *"Blues Scale,"* of course, is the musical alphabet for the Blues, just as the Major and Minor Scales are alphabets for other types of music. My Blues and Rock Breathing Patterns approximate the notes of the Blues Scale — that's why I use them to teach Blues and rock music. But playing an actual Blues Scale requires the technique known as "bending" notes.

About Bending

"Bending" means changing the shape of the inside of your mouth — mostly by using the tongue — which changes the flow of the air going through it. This changes the "pitch" (highness or lowness) of the note. Generally, bending a note means making it sound lower than it normally does.

Your Current Bend Status: Dwahs and Chokes

You've already begun to bend notes to a tiny extent. The dwah effect changes the shape of the inside of your mouth, which gives you the dwah sound. And when you get a "choked" or "funky" 2 in, you are accidently doing a partial bend.

If you can get clean, clear, single in notes, you can try to lower the pitch of a note like this: start, completely empty, on 4 in. Begin the note with your mouth completely relaxed and as open inside as possible. After a second, tighten your tongue and pull it back and down (about an inch). Some people liken this to saying "whee-ooh." If you hear the note change pitch, you're at least on the right track!

It took me ten full months to get my first bend (a 2 in). Now, most people using my *Bending the Blues* method (page 94) get their first bend within a few hours of serious practice spread over several days. Mastering this technique, like so many other things, is the work of a lifetime...

The Simplified Blues Scale and Verse

Even without bending, you can play a version of the Blues Scale that works quite well. Here is the easiest one:

In the first harmonica verse of Playalong Track 21, I use the Simplified Blues Scale to create a solo. Sometimes I just use the scale, from low to high, as in lines one and the second half of line three. Other times I create riffs from just a few of the notes of the scale, as in the first half of line two, and line three. I end the verse down low, with a Boogie Woogie variation and a double 1 in for a turnaround.

Using the Simplified Blues Scale

Just work your way up and down the Simplified Blues Scale along with Track 21, play around with the rhythm, and you can't go wrong (or not too far)!

The Real Blues Scale and a Real Blues Verse

Here's the real thing . Notice the bends on the 3 in and the 4 in — the little "b" indicates the bend.

•	•	•	•	•	•	•	•
2	**3**b	4	**4**b	**4**	**5**	6	
G	Bb	C	Db	D	F	G	

In the second harmonica verse of Playalong Track 21, I create a solo using this scale — similar to the previous verse, but with bends, and a fancy ending. I've simplified the timing slightly, to make it easier to follow. Want to play like this? My *Instant Blues Harmonica* and *Bending the Blues* will get you there.

2 **3**b 4 **4**b **4** **5** 6

2 2 **3**b 4 **4**b **4** **5** 6

4 **34**b **2** **34**b **2** 4 **34**b **2**

2 2 **3**b **3**b 4 4 **4**b **4**b **4** **45** **34**b **2**

45 **45**b **45** **34**b **2**
wwwwwwwwwww

dwah
1 **2** 2 **3** 2 3 4 3 4 **4**b 3 **4**b

waaaah   wah wah wah
4 slide 1 2 **2**   **2**bb (deep bend)

This page is *way* too hard for you to play now —
it's only to show you how the Blues Scale is used!

Playing Nicely with Others

The material in this method has already prepared you to play some Blues, rock, and folk music on the harmonica — by yourself (actually, with me and my band). Now I'll prepare you to play — or jamm, or *"sit in"* — with other musicians! This is one of the most exciting things a new harp player can do. Knowing *how* to do it will reduce stress and increase pleasure!

Jamming Etiquette

It's probably not a good idea to try to jump on stage and blow a few riffs with the Rolling Stones, when they do their next command performance at Buckingham Palace. It may not even be appropriate to start out by playing with the local rock band at the local pub — they are (we hope) being paid for the performance, you are an unknown and potentially disruptive quantity, and ego issues may be at stake. So...

How to Get Started

Begin by playing — lots — with the playalong tracks. They won't have an attitude, or kick you offstage, and they will get you used to playing along with other musicians! Then start playing with friends, in a casual setting (such as your garage or living room). Often, it's easiest to start jamming along with a single musician, perhaps a guitarist or keyboard player.

After you feel comfortable doing this, try playing with a small group. Remember that playing in front of people — even a dozen hikers around the campfire — raises the stakes a bit. So you may want to practice with your partner but *without* the audience at first, even for a few minutes before the "show."

Eventually, you may want to try to join a group on stage. Start out if possible at an "open mike" night — the band will be patient, used to playing with all levels of players, and paid to do so (which ups their patience quotient).

What You Need to Know for a Successful Jamm

If you're not an experienced musician, you can't — unless you're a world class optimist with steel skin — expect to be ready for anything the band or your playing partners want to do. So you've got to take some responsibility for what is going to be played, especially in a "performance" situation (that is, playing in front of anyone except immediate family).

You'll always need to tell your playing partners — or, even more importantly, the band leader if you're sitting in — exactly what style of music you'd like to play, and what key they will need to play in. This, as you'll soon see, will depend on the style of music and what "key" harmonicas you own.

Be honest about your abilities when you do so: "I've only been playing for a few weeks, but I can jamm along pretty well with a Twelve Bar Blues in the key of G." This isn't just a beginner thing to do. It's a realistic thing to do, for any player. For instance, when I sat in with poet/rocker Michelle Shocked, we discussed the songs for a minute, during a break beforehand. I didn't want to be trying to get the key or chord structure of a song I'd never heard, in front of an audience of 40,000!

What "Key" Harp Should I Use?

The "key" of a harmonica refers to the lowest note of that harmonica. The 1 out of your harmonica is a "C" note, so you have a *"harp in the key of C."* But you *won't* always play it in C!

If you only have one harmonica — your "C" harp — that's the key of harmonica you'll use. But the question then arises: "What key should my guitarist play in?" And that depends...

If you're playing a **Major** Scale-based song on your "C" harp, your partner should play in the **key of C** also. This is called, in harmonica jargon: *"Straight Harp"* or playing in *"First Position."*

If you are playing a **Minor Scale**-based song, Minor Jamm or Minor Blues (like *Good Mornin' Blues*) on your "C" harp — your partner should play in the **key of D minor.** Why? Because the Minor Scale you're using starts on the note D (page 46), and so is *"in the key of D minor."* This is called playing in *"Third Position."*

If you are playing **Blues or Rock** using my Breathing Patterns on your "C" harmonica, your partner should play Blues or Rock in the **key of G.** Why? Because the Blues Scale of the C harmonica begins on a G note (page 86). This is called *"Cross Harp"* or playing in *"Second Position."*

Playing Different Key Harmonicas is Easy!

Harmonicas come in a variety of keys. Generally, "G" is the lowest sounding, and "F" the highest. A new key harp will sound excitingly different, but once you've learned to play a "C" harp, you can *instantly* play *any* song you know on *any* other key harp!

But if you're using a different key harmonica, then your partners will have to play in different keys, also. The following chart will help. If you're really interested in playing along with others, and want to know which harp to use and why — read about my *Music Theory Made Easy for Harmonica* on page 95.

Want to jamm a Minor Blues on your new "E" harp? Find E in the top row. Go down the E column to the bottom (Minor) row. Tell your pal to play a Minor Blues in the key of G flat ("b" = flat).

If Your **Harp** Key is:	C	D$_b$	D	E$_b$	E	F	G$_b$	G	A$_b$	A	B$_b$	B
The **Blues** Key is:	G	A$_b$	A	B$_b$	B	C	D$_b$	D	E$_b$	E	F	G$_b$
Major Song Key is:	C	D$_b$	D	E$_b$	E	F	G$_b$	G	A$_b$	A	B$_b$	B
Minor Song* Key is:	D	E$_b$	E	F	G$_b$	G	A$_b$	A	B$_b$	B	C	D$_b$

*Important: This row is all Minor chords: D minor, E$_b$ minor, etc.

A Key Warning

Sometimes a band leader or jamming partner will ask you:
"What key harp do you have?" Don't answer! They may very
well *not* know that you need to play your "C" harmonica with
Blues in the key of G! So just reply with the appropriate key
for whichever style (Major, Blues/rock, or Minor) and harmonica
key that you plan to play, from the chart on the previous page.

Help for Your Jamming Partners

You can help your jamming partners by telling them which
chords to use when playing together. I'll provide a *"chord
chart"* for one verse of each style of the music you've learned
to play (with your "C" harp) in this method.

The Chord Charts (for use when playing with "C" harp only)

Each letter (like "G" or "Dm") represents one bar (four beats) of
music. So the chord structure of each verse of the *Dirty Dog
Rock* is one bar of **G**, then one bar of **C7**, repeated over and over.

Twelve Bar Blues: G-G-G-G-C-C-G-G-D7-C7-G-D7

Twelve Bar Rock: G-G-G-G-C-C-G-G-D7-C7-G-G

Two Bar Two Chord (Dirty Dog) Rock: G-C7

Rock Boogie: Note Pattern is G-G-Bb-C (one beat each)

The Gypsy/Rom/Flamenco Jamm: Gm-Dm-A-Dm

Minor Twelve Bar Blues (used with *Good Morning Blues*):
    Dm-Dm-Dm-Dm-Gm-Gm-Dm-Dm-A-Gm-Dm-A

All of the Major Songs are in the key of C.

All of the Minor Songs are in the key of Dm (D minor).

> Play the playalong tracks along with you and your
> partners — nice and loud — to keep everyone "on
> track," especially at first (with "C" harp only).

Harmonica Care

Your harmonica is composed of more than fifty separate parts. Attached to the comb by rivets are twenty little metal "reeds" — vibrating metal strips — each hand-tuned. Ten of them (the out notes) are on top of the comb, and ten (the in notes) on the bottom. Each reed fits into a slot in the comb, tightly enough not to allow air to escape around it, but loosely enough so that it can vibrate and make sound.

Don't eat and play, unless you're sure there are no food bits to blow into your harmonica. Even a tiny crumb will block a reed from moving, although it can probably be washed out.

Try not to drop it in the mud, but modern (non-wooden) harmonicas can be washed*, as long as you rinse all the soap off.

Don't keep it loose in your pocket — coins or keys get under the cover plates and damage the reeds! Also, hairs can get caught between a reed and its slot, so trim that mustache!

Want your harmonica to last? Don't play too loudly!
Forcing too much air through the reeds makes them go flat (sound lower than they should). When I ask you to play forcefully, that's speaking relatively. Play gentle, soft, folk music and you can use the same harmonica for decades. If you like loud, be prepared to replace your harmonica — a large, loud, rock and roller may "blow out" a harp in a single three hour jamm session or gig, if she blows with all her might...

If one of the holes of your harmonica does not seem to want to play, you may want to *carefully* unscrew the cover plates and look at the reed plates. Anything large enough to block the reed should be big enough to be seen, and *perhaps* can be gently removed. But *don't* do this unless you're the "handy" type...

* I also usually wash a brand new harmonica when I first get it.

More About My Work (and a pitch)

What I'm Most Proud Of... If you've already heard more about me than you need or want, just skip this section. If not, I'd like to say that I'm happy to have taught half a million people to blow their blues away. I enjoy holding the undisputed World's record for Teaching Most People to Play Harmonica at One Time (currently 2,569 participants, though I hope to do a big one soon). It's fun going on tv and radio every so often, and good PR for what I do. But *that* is not what I'm most proud of. Here's what does make me happy:

Many people, especially in the U.S., think of me mostly as a harmonica educator. And I am. But my academic background and training is in psychology, and my passion for the last 15 years has been in the field of *"applied cognitive science."* Huh? Cognitive science is the study of how the neurons and chemicals of the brain produce thoughts and emotions, and how these thoughts and emotions affect our words and actions. "Applied cognitive science" means that I've studied this subject, and want to apply it to real-world situations, at home or work. First to help myself, then to teach others — just as I've done with harmonica.

At first, I tried to do this through books, like *The Three Minute Meditator*. And that's worked reasonably well — it's sold lots of copies and is available in all the major languages. But in the late 1980's I began combining cognitive science *and* harmonica in my work with terminally-ill adults and children, using that strange hybrid to teach stress management and emotional intelligence. It worked so well that I branched out, and for the last five years I've been doing most of my presentations for corporate and non-profit organizations.

These clients range from Ben & Jerry's Ice Cream to Merck Pharmaceutical, from the Blue Cross to the Red Cross, and from Kraft Foods to the American Society of Forensic Lab Directors. My unique keynotes and workshops can help *your* organization to work more creatively, more effectively, with better communication and less stress! The money from my corporate work helps subsidize my work with at-risk kids, frail elderly, and people who are terminally-ill, thus I don't mind plugging it here. So if you ever need a corporate speaker... please check out **www.davidharp.com!**

"David was the most popular speaker of our three day event!" — Carol Evans, Event Co-ordination, American Red Cross

Where to Go From Here (Sales Pitch)

Perhaps it may seem as though I've been giving you a hard sell, suggesting this book or that recording, while all you're trying to do is finish *this* book! If so, I apologize. But I'm painfully aware that this book only scratches the surface of my favorite topic. Yet had I included all of the material that I think is important, this book would have been longer than *War and Peace,* and only the the larger universities would have been able to afford one. So following is a list of products that you may find of interest, if you've gotten this far!

Need to replace the recording that should accompany this book? Call or email us! Need a harmonica to use with it? Keep on reading!

The Pocket Harmonica Songbook

One of my most popular books — with more than 40 folk, rock, and Blues songs, in the notation system you've already learned. There's certainly some duplication of songs that are in this book, but lots of new ones, too. Holiday songs, Boogie Woogies, country songs, spirituals — something for everyone!
64 pages, $5.95

Instant Blues Harmonica (Ninth Edition)

Although quite a bit of the Blues and rock material

in "IBH" is the same as that in this book, *Instant Blues Harmonica* has much more emphasis on understanding how to create improvised solos using the Breathing Patterns and the Blues Scale. It also includes much more explicit information on the Twelve Bar Blues (as they relate to harmonica and improvisation). So if improv appeals to you, it may be worth your while to get this 80 page book and 74 minute CD. *Ninth completely revised edition of this Book and CD, $12.95.*

Three Minutes to Harmonica: The Video

You may have seen me selling this one on QVC —it's an even easier way to learn harmonica than this book was, with my amazing Harmonica Hand Signal Method™. Yes, some of the basic material is the same as in this book, but if you want to learn some great new riffs in the styles of Little Walter, Sonny Terry, and James Cotton in no time at all — this is the way to go! You've already got the basics. So whip through the riffs in a day, then give the video to a good friend!
Three Minutes to Blues: 70 minute video, $12.95

Blues & Rock Harmonica Made Easy

Companion volume for the *Three Minutes to Blues* video. If you prefer reading notation to seeing me jump around on video, save a few bucks and still get some great riffs! *64 pp. $5.95*

Country & Western Harmonica Made Easy

This is the musical alphabet for country music! Just learn the simplified (no bends) C & W scale, and you'll be playing along with Shania Twain and Charlie McCoy right away! *64 page book, 90 minute cassette, $12.95*

Bending the Blues

Bending is both the hardest and the most important intermediate harmonica technique. A good "bender" can add up to 16 new bent notes to a standard ten hole harp! This book and cassette (for "C", "A", or "F" harps) will teach total beginners to start bending right away. It'll teach you to use draw bends, blow bends, and even "overblow bends" in a variety of styles, scales, licks, and positions.
Bending book: 64 pages, 90 minute tape, $12.95

Bluesmasters Harmonica Classics CD

Great harp songs by Little Walter, Sonny Boy Williamson II, Jimmy Reed, James Cotton, Paul Butterfield, Jr. Wells, Charlie Musselwhite, Howlin' Wolf, and more! Available on tape (14 songs) or CD (18 songs), includes free song by song jamming hints and key chart. This and a few harps will provide you with a lifetime of learning and jamming! *BluesMasters Cassette $9.95, CD $17.95*

Music Theory Made Easy for Blues/Rock Harmonica

It's a complete music theory book for harmonica, so it's essential if you really want to play with others. Whatever your playing level, you'll be playing in new positions in minutes — with hundreds of scales and riffs at difficulty levels ranging from near-beginner to serious pro! *96 pages, $6.95*

Music Theory Made Easy: Not a harmonica book, but a more comprehensive look at music theory for any instrument, covering more styles than the *Music Theory for Harmonica* book. *80 pages, $5.95.*

Need More Harmonicas?

Pro-Level Hohner "Big River"Harps: Available in keys of C, A, F, G, and Bb, $15 each. Need a few more Hohner BluesBands? $6.95 each, key of C only. Special deal on Mojo Deluxe Harps — $5 each, C only. Other keys? Bulk orders for school or? Call us!

Rhythm! Flute! Guitar! Kids! Better Breathing!

The Instant Rhythm Kit (book and tape, $12.95) will help you keep the beat, and more! Learn Blues, rock and classical flute with *Instant Flute* ($19.95) includes book, tape, and folk flute! Or try the world's easiest and most unusual beginning guitar method for Blues, rock, folk, classical and jazz — *Instant Guitar (80 page book, 98 minute tape and "The ChordSnaffle,™" only $14.95)*. Give the gift of music with *Instant Harmonica for Kids*, aged 4 and up *(video and harp, $14.95)*. Exercise aerobic capacity with *Better Breathing Through Harmonica (especially for seniors, large print book and harmonica $12.95)*.

Last Licks

Please contact us for a complete catalog. And if you've enjoyed this book, learn what I consider to be the master skill — with my most important (and internationally best-selling) method: *The Three Minute Meditator: hardcover, 208 pages, $9.95.*

Order and Shipping Information

Order Line: 24 hour **1-800-665-6474 (1-800-MOJO-IS-I).** Please have your order ready including: your name, address, items you want sent, credit card number, expiration date, daytime phone and how you want it shipped (described below).

Phone: 802-223-1544 (M-F 10 am-4 pm EST) **Fax:** 802-223-0543

Order by email: harpstuf@sover.net

Order by Mail to: Musical i Press 323 South Bear Swamp Rd.
Shipping Costs
Middlesex VT 05602 (Sorry, no COD)

Unfortunately, our costs to ship have gone through the roof. We were actually losing money when shipping a single $5.95 book! So it's not a misprint that the *more* you order, the *less* it costs to ship!

When Total Cost of Order is:	Order a bit more? We'll pay some of the shipping!			
	Under $10	$10-$25	$25-$50	$50 & UP
These are shipped mostly via Federal Express Ground	$10	$9	$7	$5
3-day	$13	$12	$10	$8
2-Day	$15	$14	$13	$11
Next Day	$25	$24	$23	$22
US Postal Service	$8	$6	$5	$3
Canada*	$9	$7	$6	$4

*By US Post — other countries please write or email for charges.

"In his own way, from his little corner of this big ole world, David Harp is doing things to make this a better place to live."
— Charlie Musselwhite, Master Bluesman